five star mind

mind

games and exercises to stimulate your creativity and imagination

Tom Wujec

Doubleday

NEW YORK   LONDON   TORONTO   SYDNEY   AUCKLAND

Published in Canada by Doubleday Canada Limited,
105 Bond Street, Toronto, Ontario M5B 1Y3

A *Main Street Book*
Published simultaneously in the USA by Doubleday,
a division of Bantam Doubleday Dell Publishing Group, Inc.
1540 Broadway, New York, New York 10036
Main Street Books, *Doubleday*, and the portrayal of a building with a tree are trademarks of Doubleday,
a division of Bantam Doubleday Dell Publishing, Inc.

Canadian Cataloguing-in-Publication Data
Wujec, Tom
    Five star mind: games and exercises to stimulate your creativity and imagination / Tom Wujec
    ISBN: 0-384-41462-5
    1. Creative thinking – Problems, exercises etc.
    2. Problem solving – Problems, exercises etc.
    3. Brainstorming – Problems, exercises etc.
    I. Title.
    BF408.W8 1995   153.3   C95-930334-0

Library of Congress Cataloging-in-Publication Data
Wujec, Tom
    Five star mind: games and exercises to stimulate your creativity and imagination / Tom Wujec
    p. cm.
    "Main Street Books"
    1. Creative thinking – Problems, exercises etc.
    2. Problem solving – Problems, exercises etc.
    3. Brainstorming – Problems, exercises etc.
    I. Title. II. Title: 5-star mind.
    BF408.W94 1995
    153.3 – dc20   94-44988
    CIP
ISBN: 0-385-41462-5

COVER DESIGN BY FRANK SCATONI
TEXT DESIGNED IN ORBIT BY GARY STÜBER
PRINTED AND BOUND IN THE USA
AUGUST 1995

1 2 3 4 5 6 7 8 9 10

dedication

For Mikayla, whose spirit of discovery
shines brightly every day.

acknowledgments

Books become a part of one's life for a long, long time. *Five Star Mind* is no exception and its growth was helped by family, friends and professional associates. I would like to express my sincerest thanks to many people including Susan Seaman, whose caring and support provided the room to make the ideas possible; Danuta Czubak, who continually showed me how to keep focused when there were a thousand things to do; Deborah Schulde, for many stimulating ideas and for suggesting the title; Annelies Vogel, for the exploration of many notions, including the value of appreciation; Charlie Menendez, who always sees the human side; and Tony Hushion – a mentor – for showing the subtle side of creativity.

I would also like to thank Doubleday for their incredible support. In particular, John Pearce and Maggie Reeves helped keep the book moving forward. My razor-sharp editor Alyssa Diamond: thank you for working through the not-so-good ideas. And Gary Stüber, for his appealing layout of the book.

Finally, I owe a debt of gratitude to the many authors whose books about creative thinking have proved invaluable in putting together my own attempt to stimulate creativity. Indeed, there is a growing body of knowledge of creative-thinking techniques that has been developed over the past two decades. Each author brings a unique contribution to this engaging area of inquiry. I would like to acknowledge the works of James L. Adams, Richard Back, Tony Buzan, Edward de Bono, Julia Cameron, Betty Edwards, Martin Gardner, Daniel Goleman, Robert Grudin, Vera John-Steiner, Paul Kaufman, Ann McGee-Cooper, Michael Michalko, Alex Osborne, Michael Ray, Chic Thompson, SARK, Roger von Oech and Joyce Wycoff.

contents

Kayla's creative kitchen

Tom fumed. Another long day of useless paperwork, interminable meetings and now this. Stuck in traffic at 8:00 p.m. He'd be lucky if he got home before midnight. On an impulse, Tom decided to exit the highway and look for an alternate route.

As he left the off-ramp, he noticed a small bright sign winking in the distance. "Kayla's Creative Kitchen," it said. Well, at least he could get a sandwich and a cup of coffee to tide him over until he got home.

But when he opened Kayla's door, all he felt was disappointment. It wasn't much of a restaurant. Just a hole in the wall, really. A counter stretched across the small space, and behind it a trim, fifty-something woman — Kayla, presumably — sat on a tall stool.

"You're new," she said. "Can I help you?"

She must know all her regulars, Tom thought — or else, not a lot of people stop here. "Uh, yes. Can I see a menu?"

"We don't have menus."

They really were behind the times in this burg. "All right, then. I'll have a chopped egg sandwich and a coffee to go, please."

"We don't sell those."

"Just what kind of restaurant is this, anyway?" Tom demanded.

"It's not a restaurant at all," answered Kayla. "It's a kitchen — a *creative* kitchen. We feed the mind, not the stomach."

"What do you mean — some kind of day-care?"

Kayla laughed. "You could look at it that way, I suppose. But no. We bring creativity into the lives of people of all ages."

By now, Tom was starting to get interested. "Why would I want to do that?" he asked, smiling. "I'm not in the art department."

"I'll give you four good reasons," said Kayla. "First, the world is developing so quickly that you need to be creative just to keep up. Think about your work, for example. Only a few years ago we didn't have computers, fax machines, cellular phones — or cutthroat global competition. Today, people work in different ways and companies need to come up with new tactics if they want to succeed. Yesterday's approaches, techniques and practices just don't satisfy today's needs.

"Secondly, creative thinking provides us with fresh perspectives, novel experiences and innovative outlooks. It helps us grow. And when we transform creative ideas into reality, we fulfill our desire for self-expression.

"Third, creativity recharges our thought processes. The thrill of discovery injects fresh energy into our brains.

"And finally, creative thinking is fun. It's a tonic for information overload and life's pressures. Creativity grants us license to play."

"But aren't some people just naturally more creative than others?" Tom asked. "You could divide everybody at my company into two groups. Some people always come up with new and interesting ideas; the others only give you the same old thing. And what about great artists and inventors? I know I'm not as creative as they are."

"Are you sure about that?" Kayla's eyes twinkled. "But seriously — creativity lies at the heart of our humanity. Throughout history, the creative spirit has enhanced our lives. Think of how the invention of the wheel, the symphony and the computer improved the quality of human life. And if you spend any time watching children play, you'll see that they are instinctively creative.

"And there's something else. The magic of your creative powers is that the more you use them, the stronger they grow. And the more they build, the more you want to use them — whether you're drawing up a business plan or planning a vacation."

Tom thought back to his day at the office. His company could certainly use some new ideas, and as for him, anything that could inject new life into his work was worth a try. "OK," he said, "So how do I start?"

Kayla handed him a stack of what looked like recipe cards. "Here. Follow these and before you know it,

you'll be cooking up first-rate creative ideas. And with a great deal of dedication and practice, you can make it to the very top: a five star mind."

Tom looked at the small bundle. "That's it?" he asked. "Just these cards?"

Kayla hesitated briefly. "Well, there is a book that goes with them, but I'll have to charge you for that." She smiled apologetically. "After all, I have to make a living too."

Tom thought the book might come in handy. It had been a long time since he'd done any creative work — he might need a few extra tips. He paid for the book, thanked the woman and left.

As he started driving again, Tom suddenly realized that there was another question he should have asked Kayla. He pulled over, and looked for the bright, flashing sign in his rearview mirror.

It was gone.

food for thought

1

the creative urge

what is creativity?

The question Tom never got to ask was this:
Just what exactly is creative thinking, anyway? Even Kayla might have had trouble answering that one.

Creativity is a familiar stranger. Trying to define it is like trying to capture a puff of smoke with your fingertips. Although we recognize creative imagination in everything from works of art to a balanced budget, we don't know how it works. And so we tend to imagine that creativity is a mysterious and uncontrollable burst of inspiration available only to a lucky few.

Nevertheless, thinking creatively is a common experience. We experience creativity every time a fresh idea pops into our minds. And we can summon creativity when we need it. Try the following exercise: your own creative abilities may surprise you.

by any other name

Take a few moments to relax, unwind and to collect your attention.
Let your muscles relax and your breathing become even and deep.

VISUALIZE A BRIGHT RED ROSE, DETAILED, VIVID AND STEADY,
AS IF IT WERE JUST IN FRONT OF YOU.

When your image is sharp and clear, alter a single feature of the flower.
Change the color to blue.

THEN CHANGE ANOTHER FEATURE. IMAGINE THE PETALS ARE MADE OF
MONARCH BUTTERFLY WINGS. WHAT DOES IT LOOK LIKE NOW?

Continue to alter the flower's features, one at a time. Make it larger. Or smaller.
Make the texture rough and hairy. Or smooth. Alter the shape of the petals.
Into lily pads. Or diamonds.

KEEP MAKING VARIATIONS, ALTERING YOUR IMAGE AS IDEAS OCCUR TO YOU, UNTIL YOU
ENVISION AN ENTIRELY NEW FLOWER, ONE THAT NEITHER YOU, NOR ANYONE ELSE,
HAS EVER SEEN BEFORE.

Be as outrageous or as subtle as you like, but give your mind the room
to envision something entirely new. What does the creative experience feel like?

What did you do while you were thinking creatively?
How was this activity different from other types of thinking? Dictionaries don't help when it comes to answering this question. My dictionary defines creativity as originality, innovation, imagination and the act of bringing something new into existence.

Informal, everyday definitions of creativity give us a better gut-level understanding of the experience. We say that creativity is the ability to look at a problem sideways. A creative idea is a vision or insight, a moment of inspiration when thoughts suddenly fit together in just the right way. Creativity shows in a surprising solution to a problem or dilemma. Creative projects are elegant: they do the job using the fewest resources. Generally, we associate creativity with quality.

We speak of the visionary quality of creative people. They can look at the same thing as everyone else but see something different. They can look at the same thing as everyone else but see something different. An industrial designer looked at a clam shell and thought "lighting fixture." A fashion designer looked at the Eiffel Tower and thought "new hat." A chemist looked at a failed glue experiment and thought of sticky note pads, leading to the invention of "Post-It Notes." Creative people connect unrelated parts into a clever whole.

In short, "creativity" is a stew of concepts which have different meanings for different people. Nevertheless, creativity plays a role in everyone's life.

Five Star Mind will help you develop your creative gifts. It will encourage you to explore your creative spirit in new ways, to better understand what feeds your imagination, to increase your ability to invent new ideas and perspectives and to apply your creative powers to many aspects of life.

Like my last book, *Pumping Ions*, *Five Star Mind* is full of exercises, games and puzzles. There is also a new addition, my "Recipes for Great Ideas." All are designed to encourage you to participate in the creative process, rather than just think about it. We learn best by doing, and we do best by really putting ourselves on the line.

three key ingredients of creativity

You could say that there are three key ingredients which make up the creative stew. The first ingredient is *novelty*. Creative action involves doing something *new*. The capacity to conceive and produce new ideas — from shaping a novel to making a pun to visualizing a brand new flower — is vital to creative thought. You focus on coming up with something different, rather than copying existing work. In this sense, creative ideas and products don't have to be unique; only novel for the creator.

Consider the flower exercise. If you are like most people, you probably found that the more you thought about the flower, the more variations you produced. You may have started out with indistinct images, which gradually became clearer and more detailed. Over time, you probably felt more choices occurring to you. You compared the imaginary flower with memories of real flowers. As ideas popped into your head, you tried out alternatives, and evaluated whether your creation was really new. If you really enjoyed the exercise, you may have become deeply involved in your work. And if, suddenly, you came up with a startling image — tiny blue-and-white daisies with bright red stamens, or a flower made from human fingers, or a Venus's flytrap with real teeth — you may have experienced a "eureka!" — a moment of insight.

But isn't there much more to the creative experience than visualizing a flower? Absolutely. The second key ingredient of creativity is *value*. You could visualize new flowers all day long — even brand new flowers — but if your vision cannot be realized in some way, your activity has served no purpose. The person who brings a new

vision of a flower into tangible form — using paint, sculpture, words, computer animation, bricks, type, whatever — is the one who is called creative. Value makes people take notice of creative work.

To produce creative value, we use domain skills. Domain skills are abilities in particular compartments of life, such as writing, cooking, bricklaying and computer chip design. You're not going to be creatively productive as a painter unless you know about mixing colors or about the different kinds of brushes. To be really creative (in the sense of being able to produce innovative, valuable work), you've got to know the fundamentals in the area you're working on. That's not to say you can't have fun painting, but you've got to have basic skills before you're really productive.

The third ingredient is *passion*, what psychologists call *internal motivation*. This is the desire to do something for the sheer pleasure of it rather than for any prize or compensation. The opposite kind of motivation, *external motivation*, makes you do something not because you want to, but because you ought to. You seek future reward or avoid punishment.

Passion — in all its varieties — is a vital ingredient of creativity. Without passion, how could the artist dream, the entrepreneur take risks or the archaeologist travel to the dangerous site? Passion makes a person hungry for new ideas and experiences. Without the desire to penetrate, explore, unravel, contribute and tinker, the creative mind would not, and could not, push itself to new limits. But when we are emotionally involved and really thrilled, we can tap into our deepest creative resources.

novelty, value, domain skills, passion - internal motivation

7

Creativity happens when the key elements come together: novelty, value and passion. Every person has interests which stimulate their creative energy. What distinguishes creative geniuses is their attitude, commitment and willingness to dream.

everyday creativity

Many people don't see themselves as creative because they don't have a huge audience. They think that creative activities have to be the big "C" creative acts associated with writing a novel or composing a symphony. They tend to overlook the many ways in which they display flair and imagination in their own lives. Maintaining such a narrow view of creativity leads them to conclude that creativity is a rare trait belonging to poets and artists and geniuses. But the chef is creative when she makes a variation on a soufflé recipe. A bricklayer is creative when he produces a different pattern. A guard is creative when he does the rounds in less time. Often, the only difference between the big "C" and little "c" creative acts is the size of the audience.

creative cerebral cuisine

Anyone who has dabbled in creative activities — writing poems, composing jingles or even managing a project — knows that things don't always work the first time around. Getting an idea right is a process that can take time — sometimes a little, sometimes a lot.

At the beginning of the process, you have an idea of your idea, a partly formed notion of what you want to have happen. You're not entirely sure what you're going to come up with. (If you did, you wouldn't actually be creating something new.) To develop that idea, you think in different ways, sometimes mentally walking around concepts, other times focusing on single approaches.

Developing an idea is like cooking a meal.

No single description or approach accurately describes what we do when we create. Throughout this book, we'll be using a variety of metaphors and analogies to explore the many facets of creative thought. One metaphor is particularly powerful and expressive:

The "preparing a meal for the mind" metaphor highlights several types of thinking which contribute to creative ideas. As a mental chef, you plan a menu, visit the idea market and gather a variety of fresh ingredients — data and information. You clean and sort the ideas, separating the relevant from the irrelevant, then mix, blend and toss thoughts together, joining facts with hunches, speculations with observation. You cook, simmer and stew ideas, allowing juices and spices to mingle. In the end, if all goes well, you produce a well-cooked meal, ideas to nourish and satisfy.

We have many tools at our disposal in our mental kitchen — knives for peeling, cutting and separating ideas, bowls to mix them in, blenders that purée them and stoves and ovens that cook them to perfection. Preparing a meal involves knowing how and when to best use these tools.

In the following chapters, we will explore several fun ways to cook up ideas — transforming the raw ingredients of unrelated information into appetizing meals for the mind and senses.

Cultivate an appetite

Adopt a mind-set of exploration and discovery. Open yourself to new possibilities by being curious, by playing around, by focusing on what you don't know and by asking questions. Above all, give yourself permission to be creative.

Gather

Get the facts, figures and feelings which relate to your project. Collect many ingredients from many sources — local and foreign, exotic and commonplace. When you shop in the idea supermarket, remember to check for freshness.

Cut

Analyze ideas by dividing them into smaller parts. Determine the essence of problems or projects. Figure out qualities and quantities. Divide ideas into new categories. Chop them up so that you understand them in new ways.

Mix

Join, relate and marry ideas. Look for connections, make comparisons, relate your idea to others, invent metaphors and develop analogies. Trust in your capacity to be inspired by creating the conditions in your mind for new connections to take place.

Cook

Let your ideas simmer and stew. The doors to deeper creative experiences are persistence, hard work and drive. Focus your concentration by developing an inner rhythm of expression and reflection, and by striving to reach the psychological state of "flow." Know when to turn up the heat and when to let things cool down and marinate in their own juices.

Spice

Add accent and flair to your ideas. Have some fun by asking "what if" questions. Change contexts. Express your idea in a different mental language. Tell a story, draw a picture, make a model, formulate an equation or chart a map. Challenge your assumptions, break the rules and encourage that ever-present friend of creativity — luck.

Taste

Evaluate your creation. Determine how effective your ideas really are. Recognize the strengths and weaknesses. Know that ideas should appeal to the eye as well as the palate. When things go wrong, as they sometimes will, figure out what you can learn from the experience.

Digest

Take time to assimilate ideas. Are your ideas providing a balanced mental diet, or are you consuming too many mental sweets? Remember that a well-nourished intellect enjoys sustenance from all the mental food groups.

Each stage of preparing an idea — from gathering raw ingredients to tasting and assimilating the final product — represents a part of an ever-changing process. Unlike a recipe, the creative process *cannot* be a fixed procedure. By nature, creativity is dynamic and fluid, continually evolving and changing to fit the individual and the task at hand. But, by using the techniques explored in these chapters, you can create an environment in which creativity is likely to thrive.

Each chapter of this book focuses on a particular aspect of creative thinking. Although you may not necessarily apply every aspect to a given project or problem — you don't bake a salad or toss a steak — the more ways you have to cook up ideas, the more innovative your ideas become.

The preparation and consumption of ideas — like the cooking and eating of food — never ends. Not long after we have finished a large meal, we become hungry, ready for more. In this way, cooking ideas is an act of renewal, a part of the never-ending process of learning, which we can apply to countless situations and circumstances.

mental appetizers

The ideas we cook for ourselves nourish our intellect and satisfy our thirst for knowledge. Information, experiences and concepts become the staples of our mental life and form opinions, values and knowledge. The ideas we prepare for others express our unique perspective and reflect our personal tastes. Good ideas can excite, encourage and make a real difference in a world cluttered with half-baked projects.

Tip one

Open yourself to the creative experience. Accept the risk of breaking out of patterns and trying something new. Expect to have fun.

Tip two

Don't disparage your own creative abilities. Your imaginative impulses have as much validity as anyone else's, whether you're a ballerina or a bricklayer. It's what you do with your thoughts that counts.

Tip three

The joy of cooking ideas, like the art of gastronomy, is consistently fulfilling and satisfying. Good eating is the very heart of the matter.

"THE BEST WAY TO LEARN TO COOK IS TO COOK:
STAND YOURSELF IN FRONT OF THE STOVE
AND START RIGHT IN."

Julie Dannenbaum, American Chef

CHAPTER

2

appetite

hunger for ideas

inner appetite

**Recall a time, recently or long ago,
when you felt really creative.**

GO BACK TO THAT TIME AND VISUALIZE
WHAT YOU WERE DOING, HOW YOU WERE FEELING,
THE WAY YOUR BODY MOVED, HOW YOU BREATHED,
AND WHAT YOU WERE THINKING.

Spend a few moments recapturing this time.

AS YOU DO THIS, PAY PARTICULAR ATTENTION TO
YOUR STATE OF MIND.

**What images passed through your imagination?
What did you say to yourself?
How did you feel about yourself and your ideas?**

WHAT WAS IT ABOUT THAT EXPERIENCE THAT
MADE IT CREATIVE?

**Spend a few moments building up that memory of
a strong creative experience.**

the creative mind-set

"THE MIND IS NOT A VESSEL TO BE FILLED
BUT A FIRE TO BE SPARKED."

Plutarch, Roman Philosopher

Before starting to compose music, Gustav Mahler relaxed by stroking fur. Before starting to write, Samuel Johnson surrounded himself with a purring cat, orange peel and tea. Brahms received inspiration from shining his shoes. The philosopher Immanuel Kant worked in bed at the same time every day, looking at a tower through an open window with his blankets arranged in a specific pattern. Rudyard Kipling wrote only with obsidian black ink. Charles Dickens believed the Earth's magnetic field invigorated him and made sure that his bed pointed north. To get fresh ideas, Friedrich Schiller covered his desk with rotten apples. Ludwig van Beethoven poured ice water over his head.

Why would anyone perform such exotic rites as a prelude to creative work? For many people, rituals produce a specific mind-set, a particular physical, mental and emotional state in which new ideas germinate quickly, take root and sprout. Although the notion of following a ritual can seem formal and restricted, the idea of using one to change your mood is not only common, but also very practical. What happens to your mood when you take a long walk on a moonless night, when you listen to soothing music or when you lie back in a hot tub?

Chances are you relax and open up. Your mind wanders freely and you become receptive to new kinds of thought. While in this mood, you are most likely to connect to your deeper creative resources.

The feeling of creativity — whatever it may be for you — is a vital source of power and is familiar to each of us. Often this mind-set comes upon us haphazardly, like a sudden change in the weather. As a result, we can feel at our creative best at odd times; inspired ideas may come to us in the hot tub but not at the work desk.

In this chapter, we will explore several ways of getting into the creative frame of mind. You don't need to be as dramatic as Beethoven, but you do need to be familiar with your creative mood if you want to be able to summon your creative energy when you want it or need it. To create an environment where this energy can expand and thrive, we will examine ways of using your body, feelings and attention.

what is a creative mind-set?

A creative mind-set for one person may be a state of anxiety for another. What stimulates a musician may bore a novelist. In fact, there really isn't a single state of mind — a combination of thoughts and moods — which we could call a creative mind-set. However every person experiences moments when he or she is at a creative peak. Athletes call these peak moments the *zone*. Comedians call it *being on a roll*. Musicians call it *getting into the groove*. Psychologists call it *flow* or *optimal experience*. Whatever you call it, the energy of the creative mind-set allows you to become so absorbed in what you are doing that for the moment, the activity becomes the center of the universe. The outside world fades away. For the tennis player, there is only the ball; for the artist, only the tip of the brush; for the musician, only the music.

While you are in this heightened state, you operate intuitively. You naturally take risks and act courageously. You are fully present in the moment, ignoring both past and future.

Think back now to the exercise that opened this chapter. What are your favorite creative memories? Were you writing in the dead of night? Painting as the sun rose? Engaged in conversation with a stranger? Performing in front of a group of people? Doodling a drawing just on your own? Playing with your child? Making love? Quietly contemplating life?

Most people recall their creative peaks with a feeling of excitement and freshness; creative moments feel spacious because we can express ourselves freely and easily.

When you are doing what you love, you don't think about creativity. You simply act. Thought and action blend together into a single experience. This wonderful state of mind is the essence of passion. Now for a moment, think about the *feeling* of passion. To do this, think about how you really feel when you are at your creative peak. On the following list, check off what fits for you and add any items.

Physical Sensations

A tingling sensation
Slower (or faster) breathing
A shift in posture
Holding your head higher and your shoulders lower
Longer (or briefer) fixation in your eyes
A sense that you want to move
A feeling that you want to dance around
A sensation of keeping your body very focused
A sense of lightness in your chest

Mental Sensations

A quietness of the mind
A sensation of warmth or coolness
A sensation of rushing forward
A mental image of a person, place or thing
A series of rapid mental images
A sense of challenge
A musical piece playing inside your head
A sensation that you are in control
A sense that the world is laid out in front of you
An impression of ideas springing to life all around you
A sense that you are solving something

Emotional Sensations

A feeling of excitement
A sense of happy playfulness
A state of timelessness
An appetite for discovery
A feeling of inquisitiveness and curiosity
A desire to question and connect
An urge to take a risk
A wish to learn
A conviction that you are doing something valuable
A feeling of being very focused and content
A sense of safety and freedom
An impression that you are on the edge of discovery
A feeling of wonder

As the examples at the beginning of this chapter show, creative people find ways of putting themselves in the frame of mind where they get the best out of themselves. But your method doesn't have to be extravagant or complicated. The simplest way is just to *decide to change your mind-set.* You can become thrilled about something — anything you want — merely by deciding to. Once you've decided, you shift into the physical, mental and emotional posture you naturally adopt when you are at your peak.

Is it really possible to decide to be creative? Certainly! Inventive people do this all the time. Try it yourself now. Make the decision to put yourself into a creative mind-set and then visualize how you would hold your body, how you would think and how you would feel.

When you get into the habit of giving yourself permission to feel mentally energetic and flexible, you'll naturally find the optimal moods for any specific activity. What might be the most productive mind-set for drawing, will be different from the mind-set for formulating a presentation.

Since we don't have full control over our thoughts and feelings (have you ever wondered what it would be like to have full control and whether that would be a good thing?), there are times we have to help ourselves to release bad moods, distractions, worries, pressures and any factors which keep the doors to creative energy closed tight. The easiest way to open the door and release the pressures is to relax your body.

The ritual of taking five minutes to close your eyes, relax your muscles — starting at the top of your head and working down to your toes — can do wonders to restore your sense of vitality. Breathing smoothly and evenly ten times — not forcing your breath, just focusing your attention on the air passing into your nose and out again — will also refresh your system. Becoming quiet inside and allowing your thoughts to pass freely, can relax the tensions which drain creative energy.

Spend a few minutes now exploring how a visualization can relax your body and increase the psychological room in which your creative energy can flow.

Step one

Sit back in a chair, let your muscles loosen and relax, and allow your breathing to slow down, becoming smooth and even. Count 10 breaths, mentally sounding the number with each exhalation. When you feel quiet and calm, imagine that somewhere in the room you are now in, a new door appears. Imagine yourself opening and walking through the door to find yourself in an elevator. You are currently on the 10th floor.

Step two

As you gaze at the numbers, you feel the elevator moving down very slowly; with each exhalation, you go down one level — 10...9...8....As the numbers pass by, your body becomes more relaxed, your breathing becomes smoother, and your spirit feels more open and aware.

Step three

When the elevator gets to the first level, you are so quiet inside that you can feel your heart beat. When the elevator doors slide open, you find yourself in a place you want to be. It could be a workshop, a studio space, a mountain or valley, anywhere you feel like you have all the time in the world. Give yourself the time to enjoy the experience of inner leisure.

Step four

Ask yourself: in this ideal place, what would you do? Who would you like to see and be with? How would you like to spend your time? Take a mental vacation for a short while.

Step five

When you've done what you want to have done in this place, go back into the elevator and return to the top floor, counting one breath for each floor. When you are at the top, open your eyes.

Relaxation is a simple, yet very effective, way to get into a creative mind-set. It releases energy which is locked into frets, troubles and irritations. Relax those and give yourself free energy.

What if you're on a deadline and you can't relax? Oddly, sometimes just faking it works. Put your body into the position you'd take on if you actually were relaxed. In a few minutes you may be surprised to find your mood is beginning to change.

mental focus

Leonardo da Vinci liked to put himself into his creative mind-set and enjoy his penchant for ideas simply by letting his mind wander. He wrote:

I cannot forbear to mention...a new device for study which, although it may seem trivial and almost ludicrous, is nevertheless extremely useful in arousing the mind to various inventions. And this is when you look at a wall spotted with stains...you may discover a resemblance to various landscapes, beautified with mountains, rivers, rocks, trees...or again you may see battles and figures in motion, or strange faces and costumes and an endless variety of objects which you could reduce to complete and well-drawn forms. And these appear on such walls confusedly, like the sound of bells in whose jangle you may find any name or word you choose to imagine.

If we take Leonardo's cue, we can get into an inventive mind-set as easily as finding a texture in a wallpaper, in a wood-grain floor, or in the play of light and shadow, and letting our minds wander to see something we didn't see there before.

Children are the experts when it comes to being in the creative zone. They seem to live there. They look at clouds and see hippos, chimpanzees and floating bears. They stomp in mud puddles and think of meteors crashing into alien planetscapes. They look at flowers and think of sculptures. Children's imaginations roam freely because they're not constrained by adult rules of thinking. They don't know that they have to color inside the lines.

For many people, a good way to stimulate the creative mind is by getting into a puzzle-solving frame of mind.

That's different from a problem-solving frame of mind, because problems are synonymous with difficulties, troubles and obstacles. Puzzle-solving brings out the Sherlock Holmes in us.

Many companies understand the value of getting people into a fun, creative mind-set before generating ideas. The brainstorming room at the IBM Research Center in Bethesda, Maryland is filled with a collection of metal-hinged puzzles. The participants play with the puzzles before getting down to work. Other brainstorming centers use word puzzles, but the principle is the same.

In the following puzzle, the words stand for something else. For example, in the first box, the words could mean "just under the wire." What could the other ones be?

WIRE JUST	Budget △	OVATION	**SHOT**	VA DERS
ИІИІ̃Н	sitting world	hand hand hand deck	dipping	sight love sight sight sight
cancelled	H-O-P-E-S	head ache	ME AL ME DAY AL ME AL	SESAME
R ROAD A D	house stove	bopper	CCCCCCC	milonelion
SYMPHO	ONCE 10 AM	I IIIIIIII	POppD	SHAPE or	SHIP

dealing with distractions

Preparing yourself for creative work is a little like organizing a kitchen. You gather the raw ingredients. You start with a clean and uncluttered work space. And you make sure all your tools are available.

But often, despite all your groundwork, things don't go quite as planned. You sit down to start a particular project with a set agenda in mind. You have a clear image of what you need to do over the next couple of hours — and then the distractions start to arrive.

You start thinking about something other than the project. You think about the pencil, about the paper, about what you are going to do for your holiday next month. You think about upgrading the software. You think about the phone calls that you've got to make and the faxes that have to be out by the end of the day. You think about the thousand and one things you've got going. What happens? It's as if one quart of your gallon of attention disappears.

Then you realize that you are drifting. You start battling with yourself, wondering how to pull your attention back to the project. You return your thoughts to the project. Your mind drifts to the feeling of time pressure, of having to perform. A second quart of attention disappears.

Then you begin to feel uncomfortable. You shift your weight. And you shift it again. You roll your shoulders.

Another quart of creative energy disappears. If a fly comes into the room, you may not have any creative energy left at all.

Distractions — the inner diversions which keep us entertained — are among the largest drains of creative energy. Diversions keep us entranced and prevent us from tapping into our creative resources. When some of our attention is occupied by the past or future, we prevent ourselves from being focused on the present. Fortunately, reclaiming our mental energy is a relatively simple act. As we've seen, relaxing our muscles and focusing on our breath will help to center our attention.

One of my favorite ways of collecting mental energy — particularly when I feel that I have too much on my plate — is to do a mind dump. Take a piece of paper and as quickly as you can, write down any issues which come to mind. Set all of your cares down on paper. It doesn't matter how pressing or trivial each concern is. If one comes to mind, write it down. Keep writing until you have nothing more to write. When you're done, take a step back, look at your list, and acknowledge that you will deal with these concerns at the appropriate time. This activity undermines their power to distract you. Now you can give yourself fully to the creative activity you want to focus on.

cultivate an appetite

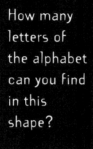

How many letters of the alphabet can you find in this shape?

Some of these questions focused on issues which curators usually don't like to include: How much does the painting cost? Has this painting ever been forged? Are there mistakes in the painting? Other questions focused on traditional artistic issues: Why did Rembrandt paint the subject? Who were the people in the painting? What techniques did Rembrandt pioneer in this particular work?

In a room next to the gallery which held the painting, the curators papered the walls with these questions (and answers). Visitors had to pass through this room before entering the gallery.

The curious outcome was that the average length of time people spent viewing the painting increased from six minutes to over half an hour. Visitors alternated between reading questions and answers and examining the painting. They said that the questions encouraged them to look longer, to look closer and to remember more. The questions helped them create richer ideas about the painting and to see the painting in new ways. Like a series of magnets, the questions attracted the visitors' thoughts to fresh ideas.

How can questions produce such dramatic results? Essentially, the questions put visitors into a ready-to-learn frame of mind by stimulating curiosity. The word "question" originates from the Latin root, *quaestio*, which means "to seek." Inside the word "*question*" is the word "quest," suggesting that within every question is an adventure, a pursuit which can lead us to hidden treasure.

When Rembrandt's famous painting, *The Night Watch*, was restored and returned to Amsterdam's RijksMuseum, the curators performed a simple, yet remarkable, experiment. They asked visitors to submit questions about the painting. The curators then prepared answers to over 50 questions, ranking the questions according to popularity.

question

In this puzzle, all 26 letters of the alphabet are present. In fact, so are the digits, one to nine. When you pose a question, you give your mind a target, a mark to aim for. The simple act of posing a question is an extraordinarily powerful way of tapping into your creative talents. Your mind naturally attempts to answer questions, doesn't it? If a question is particularly meaningful and relevant, the more interesting and engaging it becomes. In this way, a question becomes a hook for ideas. Even the symbol for a question is an upside-down hook.

Questions excite our imaginations

We don't get better ideas by staring twice as hard. We get ideas by engaging our imaginations and becoming interested, engaged and intrigued by a subject. When I start a project, I begin by jotting down the most interesting questions I can come up with. Just the act of thinking about the questions makes me want to learn more.

Questions set our thoughts in motion

Questions produce a feeling of irresolution. Like an itch, a question makes us scratch. This feeling of irresolution can be pleasurable, and explains why people enjoy solving riddles and watching quiz game shows. Irresolution is a potent fuel, a source of energy and motivation.

Questions determine our focus

The questions we ask ourselves determine the course our thoughts will take. One reason many people get stuck in their thinking is they ask the wrong questions. In an exercise I present in my creative thinking classes, I ask participants to write down every thought that pops up in their minds as they try to solve a particular problem. Occasionally, some people write down mediocre questions like: "Why can't I solve this?"; "Why is my mind blanking out?"; and "Why is this taking so long?" Their minds, faithfully answering the questions, head off in the wrong direction. If we ask better questions, like "What do I know about this problem?" and "What other kind of problem can I relate this to?" we focus our attention on where we want to go.

Questions not only whet our appetites for ideas, they provide the means of cooking up new ideas as well. Creative minds continually ask questions: a botanist, for example, walks under a tree in a park and wonders: "Why that shade of green? Why not two flowers instead of three? Why does the plant grow in this direction instead of that one?"

It's interesting to note that some synonyms for the word "question" are "conflict," "problem," and "difficulty." We tolerate conflict and irresolution in the hopes of being rewarded for our perseverance when the work is over. But there is no end to asking questions. Because there is no book of final answers, we continually formulate and refine ideas. For a person focused on solutions, answers are more valuable than questions. For a person interested in learning, questions are more important than answers.

So what kind of questions put our minds into energized states? From the point of view of creative thinking, one of the best starting questions is an *opening question*. An opening question is a question which helps to focus your challenge and usually takes the following form:

In what ways can I _____ **?**

Fill in the blank with a challenge you are facing. You might ask "In what ways can I get a better job?"; "In what ways can I improve my health?"; "In what ways can I improve my relationship with my children?"; "In what ways can I be more effective at work?"; "In what ways can I be more assertive?"; "In what ways can I produce a 15% market penetration for this game in the next year?"; and so on. Opening questions give your mind a frame of reference and a specific target for producing ideas.

Notice that opening questions are open ended. They don't ask for a single solution, but many. When you ask, "In what ways can I be more productive?" you give yourself a target which stimulates your thought.

Asking opening questions is a little like trying on a jacket. You try different ones on, feeling them for size, quality and fit. The first one is not always the best. You try different formulations, replacing words with synonyms and related words until you get a question that's just right, one that gives you the target.

give yourself a target

The more time you spend thinking about your opening question, the better your chances of giving your thoughts a clear target. And conversely, the less time you spend developing your opening question, the less likely you'll find what you are really looking for.

An opening question helps clarify what you want as the end result. It is another way of saying, "I need an idea for _____." Imagine opening questions you might formulate if you were negotiating with your spouse, searching for a new business opportunity, planning to redecorate your living room, looking to buy a new car or planning a surprise birthday party. In each case, the opening question helps establish a perspective. In negotiating with your spouse, you might ask, "In what ways can we come to an agreement over this issue?" Presumably, you won't want to ask, "In what ways can I win this argument and make my spouse feel really lousy?"

exploring the opening question

"I'D RATHER KNOW SOME OF THE QUESTIONS,
THAN ALL OF THE ANSWERS."

James Thurber, Humorist

Because your opening question is so important, you'll want to explore it, massaging and reshaping it until it feels right. To keep your mind open to wider possibilities, expand your opening question by asking "why?" Asking "why?" helps to redefine your objectives, to stand back and understand the reason for asking the question in the first place. Suppose your challenge is "How can I spend less time dealing with paperwork?"

You can then build on each of your answers:

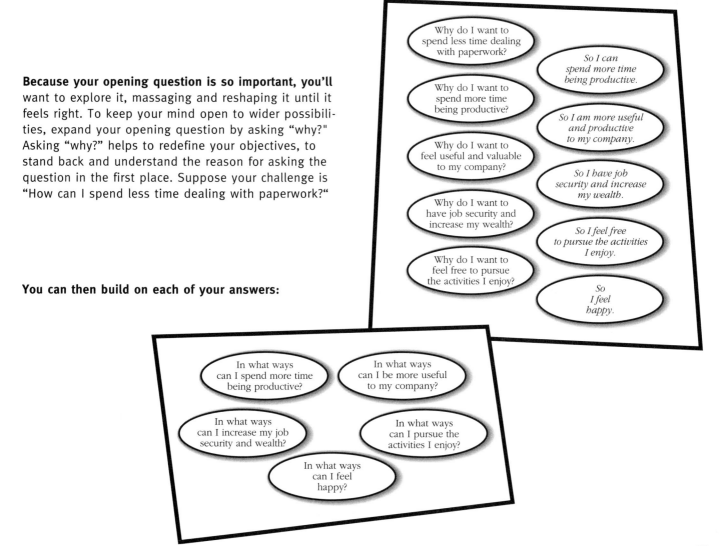

Why questions help you step up to a new level of abstraction. You can now reexamine your ideas from a new perspective. The phrase "be more useful and valuable to my company" produces more openings and opportunities than the phrase, "spend less time doing paperwork." In the end, you may decide to change the focus of your job or negotiate a different contract, rather than concentrate only on paperwork.

Stating your challenge — the very need for your idea — as broadly as possible, you place yourself as author Michael Michalko writes, "on top of a mountain from which you can view all possible approaches to the top. If you don't look at all the possible approaches, you may preclude yourself from seeing the best route to the top."

questions and wonder

EXERCISE

Take a close look at your left hand. Pay attention to the lines, shapes and patterns in your skin. Notice the arrangement of veins, the way the hairs lie. Look to see how your fingernails meet your fingers. Compare fingerprints with each other. When you have examined your hand carefully, figure out what you don't know about it. Formulate five really good questions about your hand.

How can you learn until you empty your cup?

What don't you know about your hand? Certainly there are countless details. You could have wondered how much your hand weighs or why you have lines in your palms. (Do they carry any esoteric meaning?) You could have thought about the mechanics of your hand. (How many bones does it contain?) You could have wondered about the function of fingernails. (How long do they grow in a year?) Or you could have thought about handedness. (Why do so many more people prefer using their right hand over their left?)

Besides the tangible ideas about your hands, you could have leaned toward philosophical issues. (If an open hand means "welcome" and a tight fist stands for aggression, what does a hand that's half open or closed mean?) You could have let your imagination consider fanciful notions. (What if hands were twice as large as they are now? How would that affect society, typewriters or fashion?) Or you could have wondered about the evolution of the hand. (Why did humans end up with five fingers? Why not more?)

The point of such an exercise is to illustrate how questions can also stimulate a sense of wonder, a sense of marvel over the universe. When you look at the objects around you, you are just one thought away from wonder.

There is a famous Zen story, recounted by Roger von Oech in *A Whack on the Side of the Head*, about the role of knowing, learning and wonder. A Zen student enters the enlightened master's home for the first time. The master serves tea, a tradition before discussing ideas. He fills the student's cup to the brim, and then deliberately keeps pouring. The bewildered student says, "The cup is full. It will hold no more." The master stops, looks at the student, and says, "Like the cup, you are full of your ideas. How can you learn until you empty your cup?"

We often think of ignorance as a sign of weakness or stupidity, and that's unfortunate. Though we naturally want to appear knowledgeable, the *appearance of being knowledgeable* can cut us off from learning. The Zen tradition calls this state of mind, the *expert mind*. The expert mind is the frame of mind we have when we feel we already know something. We hold on to ideas — ideas that we may have studied for years, ideas for which we earned a Ph.D. — and close the door to learning.

With *beginner's mind*, we have an empty mind, a mind which is open to wonder. While the expert mind lives in the past and future, the beginner's mind lives in the present. Someone with an expert mind barely notices a scene which he drives past every day on the way to work, thinking he knows it intimately well. But a person with beginner's mind attends to every detail. How do musicians give fresh performances after six months on the road? They remember that each performance is the first for an audience and should be as fresh for the performer as it is for the fans.

Albert Einstein once wrote, "The most beautiful experience we can have is the mysterious. It is the fundamental emotion which stands at the cradle of true art and true science. He to whom the emotion is a stranger, who can no longer pause and stand wrapped in awe, is as good as dead; his eyes are closed."

Creativity requires a receptiveness to the unknown and the unexpected, a state of mind sensitive to flights of imagination which lifts you out of the everyday. How can we adopt a beginner's mind for ourselves? Look around the room and ask yourself why the room is the way it is. Why is the rock in the fireplace? Where did it come from? How is the room painted? Why this color? Be open to any questions which come into your mind.

Gently guide your focus to the wonderful mystery of the questions.

So questions can quickly take your mind from a bored or distracted state into an excited and focused mind-set. The better the questions you ask, the richer the mind-set and mood you enjoy. What greater way to whet your appetite than by having interesting questions spontaneously pop into your head?

"WE CANNOT WILL TO HAVE INSIGHTS. WE CANNOT WILL TO HAVE CREATIVITY. BUT WE CAN WILL TO GIVE OURSELVES TO THE CREATIVE EXPERIENCE WITH INTENSITY OF DEDICATION AND COMMITMENT. THE DEEPER ASPECTS OF THE ENCOUNTER ARE ACTIVATED TO THE EXTENT THAT THE PERSON IS COMMITTED TO THE ENCOUNTER."

Rollo May, Physician

creative juices

So what makes creative people creative?
If we could look into the minds of creative geniuses,
what would we see?

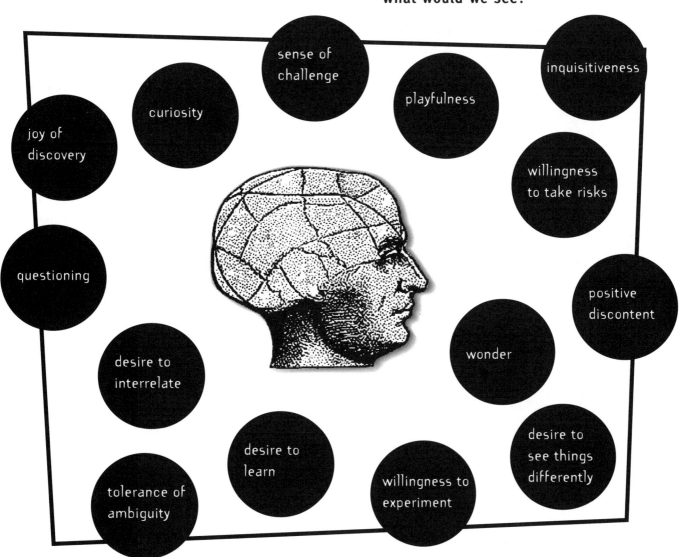

sense of challenge

inquisitiveness

curiosity

playfulness

joy of discovery

willingness to take risks

questioning

positive discontent

desire to interrelate

wonder

desire to see things differently

desire to learn

tolerance of ambiguity

willingness to experiment

Creative minds need to see, to explore, to understand, to improve and to go beyond what they already know. They are easily excited about possibilities. Creative people don't work just to achieve fame, recognition, financial gain or to get to the top of the heap. They work hard because ideas are interesting and important to them.

Creative people also enjoy a deep commitment to their work. Remember that in the last chapter, I said one of the three ingredients of creativity is passion. When psychologist Vera John-Steiner interviewed 100 creative people, she found that what they all had in common was an intense love of their work. They weren't necessarily more gifted, technically skilled or intelligent than other people. They all loved what they were doing.

What are *your* creative passions? What turns you on? What would you include in a list of five things that make you really excited and interested? If you could do anything tonight, what would you do?

Or try this one. A genie appears in front of you and offers you unlimited resources and a full year of life — a year in which you can do anything you want. At the end of this magic year, you will come back to your normal life — ten minutes from now. Nobody will know you were gone. So you are free to enjoy it as you desire. What would you do with this magic year? Where would you go? How would you enjoy your time? You have permission to do anything. What would you do?

Tap into your creative power by doing what comes naturally to you.

personal musings

Each of us wonders what life would be like if we'd made different choices. If you did something different, what might it be?

If I wrote a book, the book would be about _____.

If I produced a movie, it would be a _____.

If I painted a picture, the subject would be _____.

If I wrote a stand-up comedy routine, I would tell stories about _____.

If I composed a song, I would write about _____.

If I was going to do something nobody would expect me to do, I would _____.

If I was going to cook a meal for a dozen of my friends, I would cook _____.

If I won a thousand dollars to throw the party-of-the-year, I would make it memorable by _____.

If I designed my dream home, it would have _____.

If I designed my ideal vacation home, it would certainly have _____.

If I could be paid to study any subject for a whole year, I would study _____.

If I could spend two months anywhere in the world, I would go to _____.

If I could live anywhere in the world, I would live in _____.

If I could have dinner with anyone on the planet, I would want to dine with _____.

Musing over possibilities and posing questions are enjoyable ways to sparking your creative mind. But what about the times when you are confronted with a particular task that you've got to do? How can you engage your creative mind? Once again, questions provide a solution. Ask yourself:

"What am I really excited about?"

Answering this question will steer your attention toward the elements of the problem you can control, those which make you feel good, and which ultimately make you more productive and effective.

But can you apply this approach to such mundane tasks as washing dishes, finishing a travel expense report, typing a manuscript? You bet! Ask yourself questions which will put you into an interested frame of mind, and you will have a better time doing the job. Your answers will help you focus on the interesting and invigorating aspects of your work.

The kinds of questions which help focus take the following form: "What am I really excited about?"; "What is really terrific about this situation?"; "What will I learn from this problem?"; "How can I enjoy solving this problem?"; and "What is really interesting about this situation?" Questions such as these illuminate the creative aspects of the project.

For example, consider dishwashing, an activity which doesn't inspire creative thought. Then ask, "What am I really excited about washing this stack of dishes?" You might come up with nothing. Then ask, "What *could* I get excited about washing dishes?" You might find answers *suddenly jump* into your mind. You could become interested in the opportunity to provide a basic service. You could try to wash them as fast and thoroughly as possible. You could make a game of it. You could examine the soap bubbles, or notice how the water temperature changes. You could try to wash each dish differently. Although the job itself may not seem to be creative, any job can be performed creatively.

When starting a new assignment and you want some questions to stimulate your imagination as well as give yourself a practical perspective on your situation, try some of these:

How committed do I want to become?

The extent to which you are willing to get involved in life determines what your life will be. Undercommit, and you have no challenges and nothing to do. Overcommit, and you have too much on your plate. At the start of an endeavor, determine whether you really have the time or resources to go through with the project. If you don't, then rearrange priorities. If you do, then jump in with both feet and apply your undivided attention. Commitment is the pledge that no matter what happens, you will do whatever you need to do to reach your objective. Without commitment, life is empty of spirit and drive. With commitment, great things can happen. To explore your level of commitment, jot down the real reasons for becoming involved in a venture. Get to the heart of your motivation. Ask a series of *why* questions, until you get an answer which you can't simplify anymore.

What is the best thing that can happen?

Often we encounter people who instantly focus on problems and limitations. Visionaries focus on the possible, or better yet, on the impossible. Imagine what would happen if things turned out as you wanted them to happen.

What is the worst thing that can happen?

A good way to motivate yourself — thereby enhancing your appetite for creative success — is to imagine the worst possible consequences if you didn't act. For example, you are on deadline to come up with a new approach for an ad campaign. You submit a poor proposal which insults the clients, who fire your company, which in turn fires you. You watch your company go out of business, and your friends lose their jobs. You also don't get another job, lose your house, are forced, with your family, to live on the street, and become destitute. The more tragic the imagined after-math, the greater your involvement can become. For inspiration, my editor likes to imagine a 16-ton weight dangling over her chair. If she doesn't get the work done, the weight drops.

What is stopping me from being interested?

Just as strong positive attitudes enhance the creative spirit, persistent negative attitudes drain it away. Become aware of and eliminate attitudes which prevent you from getting into a creative frame of mind. For example, do any of these experiences sound familiar?

Not accepting anything new or different

Rehashing the same ideas again and again

Letting yourself become bored or frustrated

Starting with ill-defined objectives

Assuming that some things don't matter

Having to act in an adult way, all the time

Not bothering to really try

Being frightened of trying something new

Relying on what you know rather than learning something new

Figuring that your attitude doesn't really matter anyway

What are the negatives?

Each of us experiences discouraging times, but if we habitually allow nega-tive attitudes to take over, we close the doors of possibility. If you commit yourself to creative thinking, also make the commitment to eradicate nega-tive attitudes which prevent you from getting interested and excited. Examine each negative and substitute positive thoughts.

Step one

Form an image of the creative task ahead of you and roll it around in your mind.

Step two

Ask six questions about the task which will turn on your creative juices and stimulate your imagination. Start your questions with the following words:

1. **who?**
2. **what?**
3. **why?**
4. **where?**
5. **when?**
6. **how?**

Step three

Imagine the task completed. You might not be able to form an image of the final project, but you may be able to capture the feeling you'll have when the work is done.

Step four

Give yourself permission — permission to have fun, permission to break the rules, permission to really go wild — in your approach. After all, if you don't give yourself the freedom, who will?

Referring back to the Creative Sensations Checklist on page 17, try the following exercises.

One

Look at those words again and try to simulate the feeling right now. For example, if you wrote down "excited," then make yourself feel excited. What mental pictures can you envision that will inspire you? Are there sounds that will do the trick?

Two

Complete the following sentences:

To feel empowered I breathe ....

To feel productive I think about ....

To feel inspired I put my body ....

To feel enterprising I imagine ....

To feel creative I remember ....

To feel innovative I picture ....

Three

Imagine a person who has these qualities. Become that person. How should you stand? What should you think about?

Four

Choose the three most important impressions from your creative sensations list. Commit these words to memory and recall them whenever you need to slip into the creative frame of mind. You might make an acronym from the first letters of each of the words. The words "Breathe," "Relax" and "Concentration" could be BRiCk. Over time, however, your three impressions may change. Don't be afraid to change your approach to suit them.

the hungry mind

"THE BEST SPICE IS HUNGER."

Anonymous

What is an appetite for ideas? It's the desire to connect, interrelate, discover, search, produce, create and in particular, to learn. If a mind is already full and satisfied with existing ideas, how will it find new ones?

Tip one

Give yourself permission to be creative. Be open to the possibility of change. Be willing to try new things. Openness, curiosity and receptivity are central features of the creative mind-set.

Tip two

Keep your mind alert by asking questions. Questions couple the intellect and emotions and provide the tools with which you develop, evaluate and execute ideas. When you get stuck, ask yourself a question. Never be afraid to ask, "what questions do I need to ask now?"

Tip three

See yourself as a creative person. Bring out the adventurer, the spy, the discoverer in you. Set aside a little time each day to try something new, to think a little differently, to look at life in an unusual way. Develop the habit and your creative muscles grow stronger.

I WONDER WHY. I WONDER WHY.
I WONDER WHY I WONDER.
I WONDER WHY I WONDER WHY.
I WONDER WHY I WONDER!

Richard P. Feynman, Nobel Physicist

gather

3

collect ideas

a trip to the idea market

What is this?
Come up with five answers.

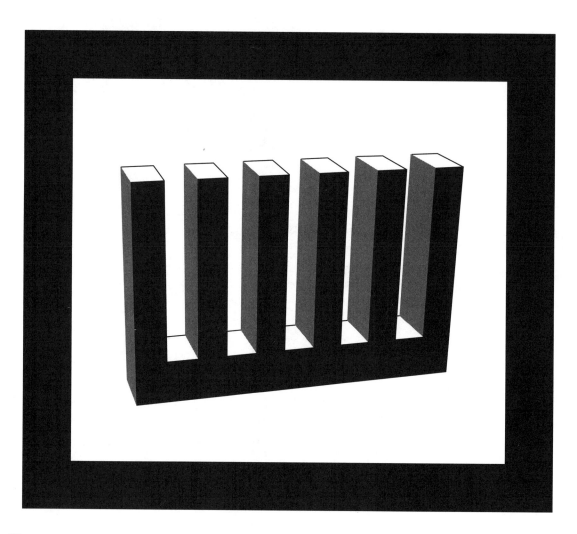

stock the mind

"GET YOUR FACTS STRAIGHT FIRST.

THEN YOU CAN DISTORT THEM AS MUCH AS YOU LIKE."

Mark Twain, Humorist

A well-stocked kitchen should have many kinds of ingredients — fruits, spices, vegetables, meats, prepared foods. A well-stocked mind should also have many raw ingredients. To supply your mental kitchen, you need to gather ideas.

Few ideas appear suddenly, out of the blue. Consciously and subconsciously, we collect, assimilate and pilfer ideas. The facts, feelings, stories and sketches we assemble constitute the staples out of which we cook meals. You can't make a meal in an empty kitchen.

How do people collect ideas? Author Arthur Hailey lived in the Roosevelt Hotel in New Orleans while researching his novel *Hotel*. Naturalist Jane Goodall lived in the African bush observing chimpanzees for 28 years. Charles Darwin traveled around the world for several years gathering the data which would eventually lead him to formulate the theory of evolution through natural selection. Before writing *Moby Dick*, Herman Melville read every account of whaling he could obtain. The development of ideas — from the most rigorous of sciences to the most expressive of arts — does not take place in a vacuum. It takes place in the tangible world of real experiences, genuine emotions and hard facts. In other words, it takes research.

Creative minds constantly take in new experiences. The questioning mind-set and burning curiosity encourage a person to become intimately familiar with many different kinds of subjects. Although gathering can be a lot of hard work, it is also a lot of fun. As a gatherer, you continually open yourself to new situations, look forward to fresh ideas and search for new possibilities. The fun part about gathering is that you *don't know* what you will stumble across. (If you did, you wouldn't be gathering anything new.)

The basic rule of thumb when gathering ideas is to pursue quantity. Search for as much information as you can, and then look for more. When you have exhausted your search, look for ideas from another source. Nobel chemist Linus Pauling once said, "The best way to get a good idea is to get a lot of ideas."

When you looked at the shape at the beginning of this chapter, what did you see? As a gatherer of ideas, you might have seen a comb for people who like squares. Or a device which produces very specific electromagnetic fields. It could be a ladder whose open ends fit into a wall with holes. The shape could be microscopic — a shaver blade for the inner ear. Or it could be gargantuan — an architectural marvel, rivaling the Arc de Triomph. What else could it be?

Normally, we don't search for many interpretations of ideas and objects because we don't need to. The elevator button is just an elevator button, and a cup is just a cup. We could spend all our time coming up with alternative ways of looking at everyday objects. But when we want to apply our creative powers, we should move beyond everyday labels and search for new interpretations. We should be open and make it a habit to keep looking.

To examine the effect of openness in creative thought, two researchers, Jacob Getzels and Mihaly Csikszentmihalyi, scrutinized how art students started their work. The researchers asked students to select and arrange objects for a still-life drawing. The most creative students — those who were most successful seven years later — played with more objects, studied them more carefully and chose the most unusual objects for their composition. These students didn't start with a fixed idea of their drawing; their visual themes emerged by handling the objects.

The reason for your complaint lies, it seems to me, in the constraint which your intellect imposes upon your imagination... Apparently it is not good – and indeed it hinders the creative work of the mind – if the intellect examines too closely the ideas already pouring in, as it were at the gates ... In the case of the creative mind, it seems to me, the intellect has withdrawn its waiters from the gates, and the ideas rush in pell-mell, and only then does it review and inspect the multitude. Your worthy critics, or whatever you may call yourselves, are ashamed or afraid of the momentary and passing madness which is found in all real creators... Hence your complaints of unfruitfullness, for you reject too soon and discriminate too severely.
Friedrich Schiller

In 1788, the poet and playwright Freidrich Schiller wrote a letter to a friend who asked for advice on generating new ideas

Over two centuries ago, Schiller understood that creative thinking involves letting go, allowing thoughts to arrive freely and rush in "pell-mell." The key to getting lots of ideas is to open the gates, to become sensitive to tiny voices and faint images in the mind and let thoughts bubble up. You'll have plenty of time to evaluate the results later.

Every person has individual ways of prospecting. A friend of mine composes musical scores for films by first relaxing his mind and then dropping his fingers randomly on a keyboard. He listens very closely to the sounds and allows his imagination to wander. A sequence of notes — as few as two or three — suggest possible melodies, textures of music, avenues of thought. He calls this process "sniffing out musical themes." In the beginning, he finds it important just to listen, search and hear musical ideas come to life in his imagination. Later, he shapes and develops the ideas into musical statements, paragraphs and stories.

Another friend of mind, a visual artist, works in a similar way. She begins by sketching without a particular image in mind and lets her hand roam the paper freely. In the free-flowing images, she sees shapes and designs, patterns within her work. When she finds an image that appeals to her, she develops that image into a realistic drawing.

There are many ways of generating ideas from different sources. This chapter will look at several methods, among them giving yourself a target, setting an idea quota, observing precisely, exercising your memory and brainstorming.

give yourself a target

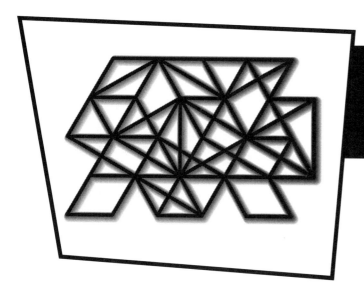

EXERCISE

Look for a hexagon in the shape.

It is amazing how selective attention can be. If you are planning to buy a new car, you will notice the options on the highways. If you are interested in a new job, your ear perks up when you hear of career opportunities. If you are in the market for business opportunities, you'll smell them out. And, if you search for new ideas, you adopt the mind-set where you're ready to find them.

People find what they are looking for. When you know what you are looking for, the image simply pops up. When you pay a visit to the idea supermarket, form an image of your target. Have a sense of what you are looking for. Declare a target and your mind will find ways of finding it.

Initially, you may not know what you are looking for. But if you have, at the very least, a sense of what would work or feel right, you will be able to recognize the answer when you've got it. You'll be able to direct your attention along the right path and sniff out the interesting ideas.

set an idea quota

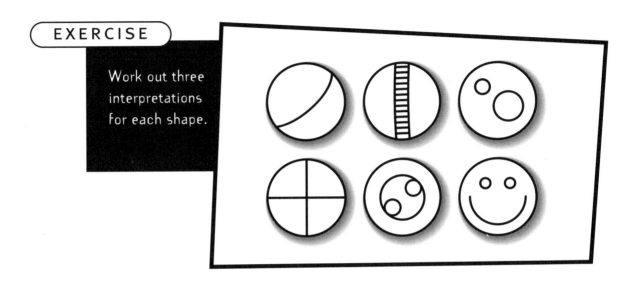

Work out three interpretations for each shape.

Encourage quantity by assigning yourself a quota to fill. If you set yourself a quota of six ideas every day for a week, you'll exercise your mental flexibility. Like any stretching routine, the first few times are the most difficult, but in a short time you'll develop momentum and new ideas will roll in as one idea triggers the next.

Pondering the shapes above may have led you to curious and unusual interpretations. You may have seen the first shape as a beach ball, a crescent moon, an acorn, a closed eye or a view of someone's tummy.

Giving yourself an idea quota encourages you to actively gather ideas rather than wait for them to appear. You may end up generating absurd or preposterous ideas to fill your quota, but you never know what gem may turn up in the next thought.

For practice, try the following exercise:

Generate five ideas for making your work desk more usable.

Invent five ways of making yourself more physically fit.

Conceive of five issues surrounding extraterrestrial life.

Determine five ways of reducing violence against women.

Make up five things you could do to make your commuting time more productive.

observe precisely

Often we don't make full use of our senses. We give little more than a passing thought to the objects and information we encounter every day. We may look, but we don't see.

Observing the world with focused attention develops the ability to study everyday objects — plants, articles of clothing, patterns in concrete pavement — and discover the wondrous. Besides providing raw ideas for ideas, precise observation gives us the delightful experience of seeing details within every aspect of an object. A flower petal becomes a remarkably intricate structure, alive with subtle shapes, patterns and vibrant coloring.

Precise observation helped the Swiss designer George de Mestral. After a hike in the mountains, he noticed the way burdock burrs stuck to his Irish pointer. Anyone else might simply have cursed, but de Mestral wondered why the burrs clung so closely. When he returned home, he examined the burrs under a microscope and saw hundreds of tiny hooks that gripped the fur. He realized that a burr fastener would be a marvelous invention. Unlike a zipper, it would not catch or jam. Although it took many years to develop the nylon counterpart, de Mestral finally developed Velcro.

To develop your powers of focused attention, choose any object — say a coffee cup — and spend a minute or so examining it very closely. Notice details: colors, shapes, textures and patterns. Close your eyes and recall what you saw. Form a mental image of the object. Then open your eyes and focus on the cup. Run your eyes across the surface of the cup, attending to more details, filling in your impression of the cup and then close your eyes and reexamine your impression. Do this several times until you know the object in a new way.

To develop another aspect of your powers of observation, choose a common everyday object or phenomenon and notice the number of times a day you come into contact with it, as well as how it affects your life. Consider water, glass, electricity, doors, the color red, smiles, motors, plastic or the number "9."

When we cultivate the habit to pay closer attention, we realize just how rarely we engage the full capacity and force of our attention. To develop yet another aspect of your powers of focused attention, attend with a different sense. As young children, we learn by using all our senses — touching, tasting, smelling, listening and watching. But in school, many of us are taught that "learning" takes place with words alone. After all, books provide the main source of ideas, teachers stand at the front of classes and speak and our knowledge is tested by way of written exams. "Research" generally means a visit to the library. Meanwhile, consider the words of Nobel biologist Albert Szent-Gyorgyi: "I owe all my results to the fact that I love life. I live it trying to observe carefully everything I see. I always study living material. I examine it by touch, I watch it and I observe every small thing about it."

Seeing fingers

Close your eyes and run your fingers across the back of your hand. Form a mental touch image of your hand, its texture, the bones and blood vessels. What would the equivalent of color be in touch?

Knowing ears

Listen carefully to the pitch of a kettle as it warms, boils and boils vigorously, and you get first-hand information about the thermodynamics of water.

Aural movie

The next time you travel to work, listen closely to the sounds around you and mentally construct an aural movie of your trip. Listen for near and distant sounds. On your way home later that day, make the movie again, listening for differences.

keep your memory active

EXERCISE

Spend one minute closely examining this illustration. When you are done, take out a blank piece of paper and draw it from memory.

According to the Greek myths, there were nine Muses who breathed inspiration into the mortal mind. The mother of the Muses was Mnemosyne — memory. The Greeks understood that memory is a fundamental resource, a wellspring of impressions into which we continually tap. Vivid memories provide valuable ingredients for the creative mind.

Although each of us has countless memories stored away in our brains, we all don't make our memories available to our creative imagination. We look to the outside world for inspiration rather than to the inside world. Say you need to generate a list of 20 different birds. Your first instinct might be to pull out a bird book or encyclopedia. But if you look within, you may find that your memory is more than equal to the task. Start by listing birds you commonly see: robins, crows, blue jays, parrots, budgies. Then start adding categories, such as flightless birds: penguins, chickens, turkeys, pheasants; birds of prey: eagles, owls, hawks; birds found in cities: pigeons, finches, swallows; endangered birds: whooping cranes, condors; and birds that just pop into your mind: hummingbirds, warblers and woodpeckers. Before you know it, your list is complete. You might try the same with a list of 20 foods, wines or cars.

Good memory is essential to the development of new ideas. Next time you are confronted by a creative challenge, try to remember if you have solved a similar problem, or read a related article, or have done related work before. Bring your past experiences to bear on the present.

memory triggers

Stimulate your memory by answering the following questions. Try to recall each experience vividly, engaging all your senses and feelings.

What is the largest animal you have ever seen? Tree? Person? Building? Hairdo? Mirror?

What is the smallest hairbrush you've ever encountered? Diamond? Camera? Computer? Watch? Face?

Describe yourself when you were 18 years old. What was important to you? How did you feel when you got up in the morning? What did you see? Who were your three best friends? What clothes did you wear? What kind of watch did you wear?

Recall several occasions on which you were traveling very fast. These could include experiences on a bicycle, in a car, during a parachute or bungee jump.

Describe yourself when you were eight years old. What was school like? Who was your best friend? What were your teachers' names? How did you spend your vacation? What did you like best about being eight? Can you remember your running shoes?

Can you remember what life was like before you could read, type or drive a car?

What was the stormiest weather you've ever experienced? Can you recall the brightest, hottest day? The darkest night? The coldest rain? Can you remember the most spectacular clouds?

Can you remember your first conscious choices?

What are your three favorite memories? What makes them so special?

What are your three worst memories? Why are they so bad?

Recall three memories you haven't thought about in years.

Three-dimensional memory

Very often when we recall past events, we flatten them into pinpoint events — dates, static images, frozen moments in time. Perspective renders them stationary. But lived experience through time is dynamic and complete with choices, concerns, uncertainties and swings in possibility. Choose an event, such as your wedding, graduation, move into your current home or first day of your current job and try to relive it in your mind. How did you feel a week before the event? How did you feel the morning of the event? What about an hour later, or a week or a month? Who did you talk to? Can you recall how things changed?

Telephone keypad

Can you draw the numbers, letters and symbols of a telephone keypad from memory?

Favorite ideas

What creative ideas have you encountered recently? Have you heard an interesting story? A joke? A way of selling a product? Does a scene from a television show stand out? A quote in a magazine article? Perhaps you were excited by a new scientific discovery.

Mental movie

As you lie in bed ready to drift off to sleep, play a mental movie of the day's activities starting from the moment you got up to the time you went to bed. Watch yourself as if you were the lead character.

visual brainstorming

One terrific way to dig into your personal treasure trove of ideas is to brainstorm visually. In the center of a blank sheet of paper, write down a word which lies at the heart of your idea. Then, drawing outward from this word, jot down any related fact, impression or image which might be relevant to the topic. As you jot down your thoughts, you create a structure which graphically illustrates the idea. For example, the subject of water might produce the following idea map.

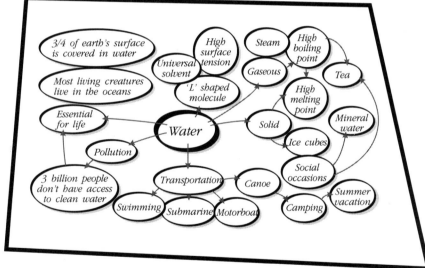

Visual brainstorming gives you a chance to let ideas run wild: you can branch out in any direction, follow any association, connect directly with your intuition. You don't need to follow any predetermined path or outline. As thoughts slip through your consciousness, write them down. Relax any urge to censor or hold back ideas.

Trust your imagination to come up with an intelligent portrait of the subject.

Visual brainstorming invigorates the imagination. Like a Zen painting which begins with a single brush stroke, these visual idea maps are spontaneous creations, snapshots of our associations of the moment. Breaking old patterns and devising new ones releases energy, and lets us see the world in a different way.

Idea maps are terrific for planning all sorts of things, from vacation trips to outlines for books. The more options you can put down, the more material you have to work with.

Idea maps help you communicate with yourself. So it's okay if the relationships are confusing or apparently unrelated. It can be as messy or as clear as you like. The important thing is that you can read it and you give yourself a period of concentrated thought.

Mapping ideas triggers mental sparks. Sometimes they need to be tended and fueled with more information before they flare into ideas. And sometimes, these tiny fires smolder for days, weeks or months before they blaze.

For fun and practice — after all brainstorming is a skill that improves with practice — choose one of the following subjects and produce an idea map. Write down as many connections and relationships as you can build from the word. Work quickly. Be open to any suggestion that comes to mind. Keep moving, keep moving, keep moving.

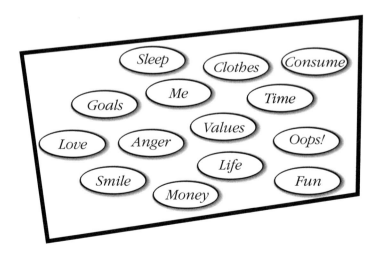

Step one

In the center of a piece of paper, write down a word or phrase which expresses the idea you want to think about. Take a few minutes to contemplate the subject.

Step two

Produce an idea map starting with this word. Write down associations as quickly as they come to you. Use your map to structure your ideas and thoughts. Keep writing until you run out of ideas.

Step three

Let your mind focus on big issues. If you are mapping the idea of, say, communication at the office, then think about the nature of communication, what it means and what it stands for. Then focus on details. What are specific, concrete, measurable details which connect to your idea?

Step four

When you feel that you've really explored the issue, select three key ideas from your idea map. Formulate each one as a problem statement, an insight or an approach. Set them aside for future use.

group brainstorming

The expression *brainstorming* was coined by the American industrialist Alex Osborne in the 1950s. In his classic text, *Applied Imagination*, he described several ways to conduct brainstorming meetings to help managers produce more innovative ideas. Brainstorming meetings were generally run by facilitators, individuals who didn't actually add to the stock of ideas, but who managed the *flow* of ideas. They guided the groups to generate as many ideas as possible and build up healthy group dynamics.

Consider a brainstorming session in which the task was to search for ways to deter people from watching television.

Aim for lots of ideas

The group produced over 150 ideas. *Ideas are like seeds. Not all of them will survive, so you need to plant a lot of them.*

Aim for different kinds of ideas

The group created television commercials designed to discourage television watching. They devised brochures promoting reading. They suggested parties at which people get together, socialize and discuss the drawbacks of television. Rambling through possibilities increases the chances of exposure to new influences. Often the block to a creative solution is a narrow-minded concentration within a single frame of reference. A person who combines several frames of reference and makes connections will be more likely to make the creative breakthrough.

Here are a few more tips on how to get the most out of a brainstorming session:

Stay loose

People generate more ideas when they have fun. They feel free to say anything and to spin ideas off each other. One person suggests putting locks on a television, causing another to think of attaching a timer to the power button, causing a third to think of charging for viewing time, causing a fourth to suggest taxing the amount of time the television is watched. This loose, flexible working style greatly improves your chances of generating a quantity of creative material. Staying loose allows you to express the half-formed ideas swimming at the edge of your consciousness. Welcome them with open arms.

Don't judge

We usually think of judgment in the context of negative criticism. And we've all had the experience of having an idea knocked down before we had the chance to develop it. Negative criticism brings the free flow of ideas to a screeching halt. When collecting new ideas and opinions, remember that judgment stops the flow and breaks the rhythm. Realize that new ideas are like delicate bubbles. They can be popped by a sneer or a yawn, or blown away by a quip or frown.

Write down everything

Choose a group scribe, whose job it is to capture all the team's ideas. Pick someone who can write fast! Write on large sheets of paper. Cover the walls with these sheets so each person can see every idea. In this way, the participants can easily add to and modify previous ideas.

Be outrageous

Have fun. Be off the wall. Go for outlandish ideas. Often the best ideas come from the weirdest seeds. One person's idea to blow up people's television sets can lead to the idea of a safety switch on a bomb which can lead to the idea of a device which needs to be held by a television viewer. Let go of the device and the television turns off. The point of gathering is to collect as many ideas as you can. You'll have plenty of time to sort through and evaluate them later.

Evaluate

When its time to select specific ideas or narrow the group's focus on the best ideas, have the participants use markers or adhesive dots to select their favorite three ideas on the sheets of paper. Very quickly you'll have a sense of the most popular ideas.

Group brainstorming puts you into a playful, loose state where ideas flow freely. You don't expect to make use of every idea you discover or produce. But you do consider every idea tabled. Chances are that 99 out of 100 won't amount to anything — but the 100th idea might change the world.

get interested

The Italian industrial designer, Luigi Colani, begins work on a project by taking country walks, observing nature's patterns, shapes and operations. His designs appear remarkably organic: propellers look like flower patterns, bicycle seats resemble leaves, cars appear as streamlined sea creatures. Few of his creations have straight lines. Colani believes the more nature he puts into his designs and the less "Colani," the more comfortable, cost efficient and charming to the eye the final products will be.

Colani is not the only inventor to draw ideas from nature. In the nineteenth century, Marvin Stone modeled the lemonade drinking straw from a hollow tube of rye grass. The U.S. army developed some of its concealment tactics by analyzing the patterns of moths, chameleons, butterflies and countless other insects. Architect Eero Saarinin, who believed that buildings should possess bold unity, got the inspiration for New York's TWA airline terminal by looking at a grapefruit.

Raw ingredients for ideas lurk everywhere: in conversations, television shows, books, cloud patterns, graffiti, restaurant menus, children's toys and so on. The experienced mental chef knows how to incorporate many ingredients. We can search for lots of ideas in lots of places — not just in libraries, but in familiar objects and everyday experiences. Don't just look for knowledge in books, but in things themselves. As Thomas Alva Edison — who held 1,093 patents — said, "Make it a habit to keep on the lookout for novel and interesting ideas that others have used successfully. Your idea has to be original only in its adaptation to the problem you are working on."

"EVERY REALLY GOOD CREATIVE PERSON IN ADVERTISING HAS ALWAYS HAD TWO NOTICEABLE CHARACTERISTICS. FIRST, THERE WAS NO SUBJECT HE COULD NOT EASILY GET INTERESTED IN, SAY EGYPTIAN BURIAL CUSTOMS TO MODERN ART. EVERY FACET OF LIFE HAD FASCINATION FOR HIM. SECOND, HE WAS AN EXTENSIVE BROWSER IN ALL SORTS OF FIELDS OF INFORMATION. FOR IT IS WITH THE ADVERTISING MAN AS WITH THE COW: NO BROWSING, NO MILK."

James Webb Young, Advertising Executive

expose yourself to good information

According to architect and publisher, Richard Saul-Wurman, a weekday edition of the *New York Times* contains more information than the average person was likely to encounter in a lifetime in seventeenth-century England. Over the course of a single calendar year, the typical North American reads 100 newspapers and 36 magazines, watches almost 2,500 hours of television, listens to more than 700 hours of radio, buys 3 books and 20 records, fills out 3,000 notices, forms and memos and talks on the phone for over 60 hours. How much time did we spend selecting this data?

The information we consume determines the health and contents of our mind. Select a balanced and varied diet of data and your intellect will have the resources to make better decisions and to generate better ideas.

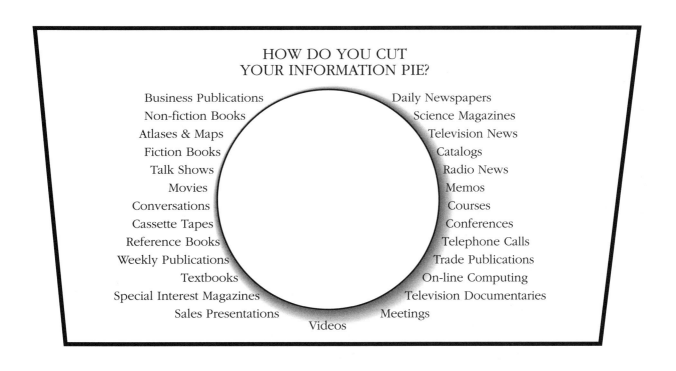

HOW DO YOU CUT
YOUR INFORMATION PIE?

Business Publications
Non-fiction Books
Atlases & Maps
Fiction Books
Talk Shows
Movies
Conversations
Cassette Tapes
Reference Books
Weekly Publications
Textbooks
Special Interest Magazines
Sales Presentations
Videos

Daily Newspapers
Science Magazines
Television News
Catalogs
Radio News
Memos
Courses
Conferences
Telephone Calls
Trade Publications
On-line Computing
Television Documentaries
Meetings

Take an active approach to reading:

Ask, "What will this do for my ideas?"

Before you read a book, ask: "Will this provide a good exercise for my creative mind?" Read books from a broad range of subjects.

Keep notes

Every good book will trigger insights and special thoughts. Keep them alive by taking notes.

Outline

George Bernard Shaw made a practice of writing an outline of a book before he read it. Sometimes after reading the first half of a book he would write an outline of the second half. See what happens if you try this exercise yourself.

Solve problems

When reading non-fiction books, think up solutions before they are revealed. Search for patterns. Compare what you are reading with other material you've read. Are there ideas you can apply to your life?

Read alternative material

Explore literature you might not normally read, such as the *Utne Reader* or the *Whole Earth Catalog*. Find points of view which are different from those you are familiar with. Read women's magazines, men's magazines, teenage magazines, children's magazines. Consider some publications which lie outside the mainstream such as: *The Journal of UFOs*, a believers' view of unidentified flying objects; *Co-op America Quarterly*, a publication for creating a just and sustainable society; *Future Sex*, which explores the fusion of sex and technology including virtual reality sex; *Clean Yield*, the socially responsible investment newsletter; and the *Privacy Journal*, which tracks issues like confidentiality of records, lie detector tests, electronic surveillance and the suppression of free speech.

Try these approaches to broaden your search for ideas:

Draw from a different area

If you are looking for new ways of computer networking, go to a field and search for flowers. If you're looking for information on business management, visit a children's day-care. If you're looking for inspiration for book design, go to a museum and look at butterfly wing patterns. Give yourself permission to look for ideas anywhere: in mythology, in musical history, in road maps or in bicycle repair shops.

Personal contacts

Who are the most stimulating people you know? Conversations and exchanges of ideas with genuinely inspiring individuals are a constant source of replenishment. The sparks of thought generated by one mind set sparks flying in another.

Work outside your area

Many inventions have been developed by individuals working outside their professions. Consider the professions of the creators of the following inventions — you don't have to be an expert to produce terrific ideas.

Kodachrome Film	—	Musician
Ballpoint Pen	—	Sculptor
Pneumatic Tire	—	Veterinarian
LP Record	—	Television Engineer
Automatic Telephone	—	Undertaker
Parking Meter	—	Journalist
Penicillin	—	Chemist
Airplane	—	Bicycle Mechanic

Travel

Of all the trips you have ever taken, short or long, which has done the most to stimulate your imagination? What factors made it a stimulating trip: the museums, the people, the different languages or the fact that you no longer were in your usual routine? Travel — particularly in foreign countries — stimulates the imagination like no other activity.

Produce a kit of ideas

The experience kit — developed by the creativity consultants *IdeaScope* — is used to shift the perspective of executives. For a well-known maker of laundry detergent, the experience kit included samples of the competitors' products, a diary for recording when the executive's own home did laundry in a week and how large the loads were, an address of a local Laundromat, which each had to visit for one hour and a very dirty shirt which each person had to wash and wear to the brainstorming session. Long-time executives who used the experience kit said they saw their products in a whole new light. Imagine that you are a creative inspirer, responsible for putting together experience kits to help executives brainstorm. What items would you include for a photocopier manufacturer? A portable computer repair shop? A candy exporter? Your own business?

Break routine

Expose yourself to different information and impressions (and sharpen your powers of observation) by breaking routine. Do something every day. Write down some of the habits you've got, shift them and see what happens.

- Go to bed earlier (or later)
- When you go to work, take a longer route than usual.
- Walk slightly faster (or slower) than usual.
- Go to lunch with someone different.
- Strike up a conversation with someone you normally avoid.
- Try a new restaurant.
- Read a different newspaper.
- Listen to different radio stations.
- Watch different television shows.
- Choose a different book to read.
- Have tea or juice on your breaks rather than coffee.
- Go in to work half an hour earlier.
- Part your hair on the other side.

Routinely take breaks

Expose yourself to new ideas by building in periodic breaks in your work schedule. Find a quarter of an hour to wander around, replenish yourself and find something interesting.

Every day take a 15-minute break to relax and open yourself to new stimuli

think aloud

Conversation is the most enjoyable way of communicating. Conversations are organic; they grow and develop along unexpected paths; they take unexpected turns; they allow us to build ideas cooperatively and bring new thoughts to life.

Conversations give us a chance to refine ideas of which we previously had only a vague concept. Ask your best friend what he or she thinks about the nature of good, or about the origin of life on the Earth, and you get a chance to formulate opinions which you've not considered before. We clarify ideas by putting them into words.

Why are good conversations fertile soil for ideas to germinate? Where else do you have the freedom to add, interject and question? Conversations don't need to be logically constructed. We spontaneously jump from one topic to the next, encouraging quick turns of thought, free associations and plenty of give-and-take. We take cues from the listener and repeat ideas, simplify, add more detail when questioned, support our notions when challenged. This unstructured freedom gives us permission to construct ideas on the fly.

The word "communication" comes from a word which means "share." When we pass ideas back and forth we create a rhythm in which one remark stimulates another. An off-hand comment prompts a distant memory. Conversations divide and unite unrelated concepts into relevant thoughts. Dialogues become collaborations, a concert of thought, the creation of a common understanding.

Of course, conversations can also quench ideas. When a lack of symmetry exists between two people — such as occurs when one person holds greater power or is following a hidden agenda — conversations lose their ability to convey new thought. One person feels the other should subscribe to his point of view, and concentrates on convincing the other. When we stop listening, we lose the opportunity to learn.

memory triggers

Good communication not only involves expressing your point of view clearly and thoughtfully, but also listening to what other people say. Since we tend to recall only a small portion of what we hear, we need to be able to tune our mental inputs. Here are some tips for developing listening skills:

Listen

Ralph Waldo Emerson once said, "In good conversations, parties don't speak to the words, but to the meaning of each other." Concentrate on what the other person is attempting to convey, not on how you plan to respond. Judge content, not delivery. Listen for key ideas.

Bias

Notice your preconceptions and personal prejudices. Are you misinterpreting what the other person is saying? Try to be impartial and objective.

Rhythm

Don't break in, sideline or otherwise interrupt the other person's flow of ideas. Finishing a person's sentence has subtle but definite psychological effects. Offer feedback by acknowledging comments and by maintaining eye contact.

Space

Realize the role of silence in the exchange of thoughts. When a person finishes a sentence, pause for a moment. Silence provides a time to reflect. Even though no words are exchanged during a pause, communication has not ceased. During silence, attend to nonverbal communication: the dialogue of facial expressions, movements, shifts in postures, changes in breathing. Open your channels of communication beyond words.

Keep active

Keep your mind and your body language alert. Concentrate effectively by mentally assessing, anticipating, summarizing and challenging. Weigh the evidence. Listen to the tone of voice and listen between the lines.

store your ideas

"THE HORROR OF THAT MOMENT, EXCLAIMED THE KING,
I SHALL NEVER, NEVER FORGET!
YOU WILL, THOUGH, THE QUEEN SAID, IF YOU DON'T
MAKE A MEMORANDUM OF IT."

Lewis Carroll, Mathematician

Once you've collected food for your kitchen, you put it away — so that it will stay fresh, and so you'll know where to find it. Perishables go into the refrigerator, cans go in the cupboard. What do we do with ideas? Proficient idea generators keep their ideas organized in volumes of journals.

Leonardo da Vinci kept remarkable notebooks of sketches, inventions, observations of nature and philosophical ideas. His desire to maintain these notebooks was so strong that he mastered the art of writing backward "to protect his innovative ideas from hostile authorities." Leonardo's extraordinary abilities allowed him to write and design pages at the same time.

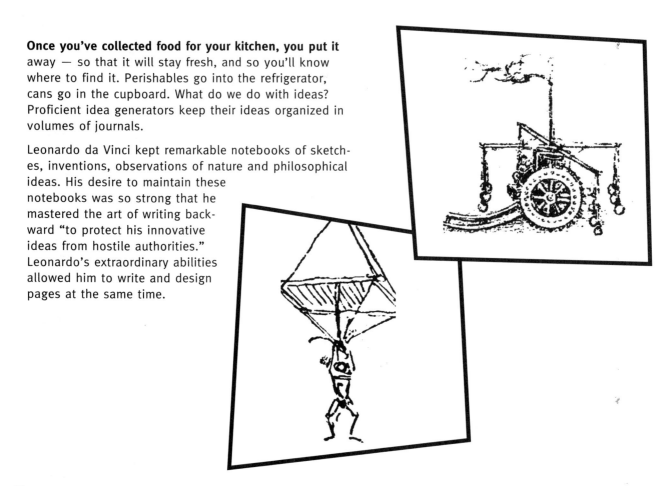

For many imaginative people, journals are an important part of daily life. Ludwig van Beethoven always carried music paper with him. His notebooks included "concept sketches," diagrams which charted the structure of his musical creations. Some of Beethoven's notebooks were used exclusively for working through and testing out variations of a new theme.

An idea journal is the only remedy for our faulty memories. If there is one key idea you should take away from this book, it is this:

Write it down or you'll forget it!

Journals provide a safe home for our musings. Insight is transient and slips quickly from consciousness. Francis Bacon understood this when we wrote, "A man would do well to carry a pencil in his pocket, and write down the thoughts of a moment. Those that come unsought for are commonly the most valuable, and should be secured, because they seldom return." The palest ink lasts longer than the strongest memory.

Journals encourage us to keep active. The word "journal" is derived from the Italian word "giorno," meaning day. The daily act of adding to your reservoir of ideas keeps your mind committed to exploration. A journal provides you with a history of your ideas, a record of your personal explorations and a snapshot of your development. You don't realize how many good ideas you have until you begin to record them. As you read them over, these ideas trigger even more ideas.

The creative urge strikes rarely enough: a journal will make you ready to record inspiration. As soon as an idea comes to you, put it into a tangible form. Write a note, sketch a picture. If you don't, how will you keep it from disappearing?

"LOOK SHARPLY AFTER YOUR THOUGHTS.
THEY COME UNLOOKED FOR,
LIKE A NEW BIRD SEEN IN YOUR TREES, AND,
IF YOU TURN TO YOUR USUAL TASK, DISAPPEAR."
RALPH WALDO EMERSON, U.S. ESSAYIST, PHILOSOPHER AND POET

gathering

"THE ARTIST IS A RECEPTACLE FOR EMOTIONS THAT COME FROM ALL OVER THE PLACE; FROM THE SKY, FROM THE EARTH, FROM A SCRAP OF PAPER, FROM A PASSING SHAPE, FROM A SPIDER'S WEB...A PAINTER PAINTS TO UNLOAD HIMSELF OF FEELINGS AND VISIONS."

Pablo Picasso, Painter

The more information you gather, the greater the pool of resources you can bring to the formulation of new ideas. Research sets the stage for the creative encounter.

Tip one

Add diversity to your store of ideas by looking outside your sphere of expertise. Go somewhere new and bring something different back to your mental kitchen. You can do this physically, by traveling to an unusual (for you) destination, such as a hardware store or a furniture manufacturer, or by taking a walk in the park. Alternatively, you might choose to make your expedition a mental one, by studying a new subject and gaining an intimate understanding of it, through books, articles and reports.

Tip two

Look for ideas that are inside you, stored in your memory. Think of events and experiences from your past that might have bearing on the project you're working on now; try to remember the details and apply them to your current situation. Can what you were doing five or ten years ago help you in your work today? Remember conversations with your dad, your sister and your seventh-grade teacher.

Tip three

Look to nature for ideas. Our planet is endlessly fascinating, and chances are nature has already done something which relates to your idea. Search among the animal, vegetable and mineral worlds for concepts that might work for you.

Tip four

Assemble an experience kit. Gather together a few items which relate to your subject and keep them around you for a while. Sometime, when you least expect it, they may trigger an important discovery.

Tip five

Record your ideas — be they notes, sketches or musical passages. Keep them in an organized fashion. Remember, if you don't do anything with your ideas — if you don't shape them into reality — they will have done little to serve you.

cut

4

analyze ideas

slice and dice

**What is the next shape
in this sequence?**

cutting up ideas

"WE THRIVE IN INFORMATION-THICK WORLDS BECAUSE OF OUR MARVELOUS AND EVERYDAY CAPACITIES TO SELECT, EDIT, SINGLE OUT, STRUCTURE, HIGHLIGHT, GROUP, PAIR, MERGE, HARMONIZE, SYNTHESIZE, FOCUS, ORGANIZE, CONDENSE, REDUCE, BOIL DOWN, CHOOSE, CATEGORIZE, CATALOG, REFINE, ABSTRACT, SCAN, LOOK INTO, IDEALIZE, ISOLATE, DISCRIMINATE, DISTINGUISH, SCREEN, SORT, PICK OVER, GROUP, PIGEONHOLE, INTEGRATE, BLEND, AVERAGE, FILTER, LUMP, SKIP, SMOOTH, CHUNK, INSPECT, APPROXIMATE, CLUSTER, AGGREGATE, OUTLINE, SUMMARIZE, ITEMIZE, REVIEW, DIP INTO, FLIP THROUGH, BROWSE, GLANCE INTO, LEAF THROUGH, SKIM, LIST, GLEAN, WINNOW WHEAT FROM CHAFF, AND SEPARATE SHEEP FROM THE GOATS."

Edward R. Tufte, Statistician and Cartographer

The act of gathering ideas produces a wealth of raw material. To develop this feast of possibilities further, the imaginative mind takes the next step of analyzing the material — sorting, selecting, editing and organizing the data.

We usually think of analysis as a cold, impersonal activity, occurring in the basements of research institutions or in psychologists' offices. But analysis is a dynamic process that can take a myriad of forms. The word "analysis" is derived from a Greek word meaning to divide into parts, to loosen or to dissolve. In this sense, analysis is the act of separating a whole into component parts; by chopping up information with mental knives and cleavers, the subject becomes clarified.

This "dividing into parts" can be put to any number of uses. You can use it to examine the benefits and

drawbacks of a career move. Or to track information flow in a large corporation. Or to decide the best way of arranging your wine collection. All complex systems, like the human body, the earth's atmosphere, Mozart's *Jupiter* symphony and Japanese foreign policy, are better understood by slicing big things into small things.

Analysis is the carving knife in your mental kitchen. Using it allows you to peer inside a situation and examine it more closely; and seeing the component parts leads you to new insights and fresh ideas.

Return to the opening exercise for a moment. How did you do with the puzzle? If you look at the puzzle in just the right way, the answer emerges suddenly. Ask yourself if the shapes remind you of something. Can you connect them to anything you already know? Could they stand for letters, a new kind of alphabet, numbers of some kind? Mentally step back for a moment, shift your focus and you may see the numbers one to seven. Look again. Each number is merged with a flipped copy of itself. So the next shape should be a double eight:

Analytic knives have many functions. They remove the extraneous, chop away the inconsequential and leave the essential. The analytic knife should feel solid, balanced and have a comfortable, secure grip. Its sharp blade should make you want to cut.

give yourself a target

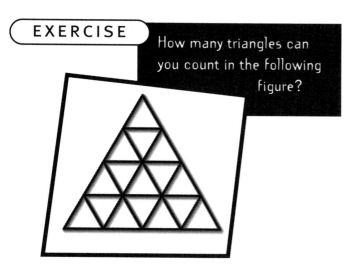

EXERCISE

How many triangles can you count in the following figure?

When we think of a problem or a situation, we usually consider it as a solid entity, a single thing. But just as a house consists of many rooms, and each room has many parts, every situation in need of creative attention has its own set of components. To generate new ideas, identify the elements and focus on each one at a time in its turn.

Say you wanted to improve your health. You wouldn't try to improve your health all at once. You would identify the many aspects of health — metabolism, nutrition, physique and so on — and see what you could do to add vigor to each — one at a time.

When you are creatively analyzing a subject, you've got the opportunity to identify and focus on many kinds of constituent parts. When you first examined the triangle mesh on the previous page, you might have seen 16 equal-sized triangles. Add the large bounding triangle and you can count 17. Add triangles of intermediate size and you will count 27. The more ways you have of dissecting your problem, the more attributes you will be able to find, alter and improve upon.

How do you search for attributes? To start, just write a list of characteristics without worrying about how accurate or comprehensive the list is. Trust in your intuition to find the characteristics that will help you explore and sort through your challenge.

You can also guide your search by breaking an object's features into categories:

Physical attributes

Consider the weight, height, width, breadth, structure, order, sequence, pattern, texture, color, speed, degrees of movement, odor, taste and sound.

Temporal attributes

What is the origin, history, present use, future use and final demise of the object?

Manufacturing attributes

How is the object conceived, prototyped, manufactured, marketed, transported, sold and used?

Psychological attributes

How does the object make you feel? Happy, sad, indifferent, thankful, impressed, wanting, satisfied?

Cultural attributes

What are the politics surrounding the object? Are there any prohibitions or restrictions on its use? What meanings does the object have? To whom? Is the purpose and function of the object the same to everyone?

Consider some features of a camera:

- **Winding Mechanism**
- **Focal Length of Lens**
- **Camera Grip**
- **Exposure Meter**
- **Lens Aperture**
- **Shutter Speed**
- **Flash**
- **Film**

To invent a better camera, focus on each attribute and try to improve upon it. Ask yourself the questions, "In what ways can this be improved?" and "Does this really have to be this way?"

Over the past 20 years, Japanese camera manufacturers have raced to improve their cameras. They have developed the following improvements:

Add-on motor drives to advance 35 millimeter film. Fast drives can reach speeds of up to 15 frames per second, ideal for sports events. Many consumer cameras have built-in winders, simplifying picture taking.

Auto focus lenses electronically adjust the sharpness of a photograph by sending infrared signals or by using contrast analyzers.

Zoom lenses allow photographers to photograph close-ups or broad vista without changing lenses.

New body designs move away from the standard 35 millimeter camera body design to those which look like movie cameras with a single grip.

New exposure meter designs use microprocessors to automate the event, even using voice synthesis to tell if the light is too bright or too dim.

Plastic lenses are lighter and less expensive to manufacture.

Vertical plane shutters move faster by traveling up and down the film plane rather than across it.

Internal flashes activate automatically if there is insufficient light.

Many film types allow photographers to select black-and-white image, color slides or color prints after they have taken the photographs. New technology removes the film entirely, producing an electronic image which can be processed by computer.

If you tried to improve a camera by thinking of it as a single entity, you might have overlooked some possibilities. What if you improved everything but the lens or the battery or the weight?

Many manufacturers use the slice and dice technique of creative thinking when modifying their products. The Swedish tool manufacturer AB Bacho Tools developed a screwdriver handle, with space for two hands, that has won many design awards. The University of Hawaii developed a telescope design which divided the large main mirror into several smaller and cheaper tiled mirrors which are computer controlled to act as a single large mirror. Apple computer developed a laptop computer with a built-in mouse.

This approach of chopping up big things into little things works at all levels of activity, from industrial product development to figuring out how to make a more memorable staff Christmas party. Think of how you might divide these large issues into smaller ones:

Writing a letter to someone who has just lost their job

Helping a teenager decide on a university

Deciding on the best way to lose weight

Embarking on a romantic relationship

Teaching a ten year-old to juggle

Often you can improve an idea by making a number of small variations. Individually, each change may not be significant, but together, the changes may add up to produce a remarkable evolution.

The more you can divide a problem into its components, the more hooks you have for exploring and solving the problem. Look at these five figures.

Which is the widest?

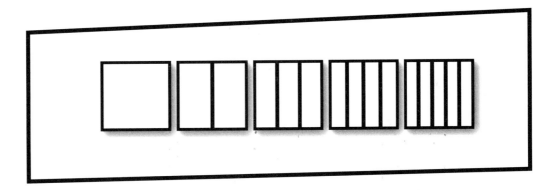

In fact, the figures are identically sized squares. But they *look* larger when you divide them. Similarly, as you cut and divide your project into smaller pieces, your perception of it changes.

Step one

Write down your problem, situation or challenge in the center of a piece of paper. Using an idea map, jot down several important attributes. If, for example, your challenge was to improve a chair, write down ten features.

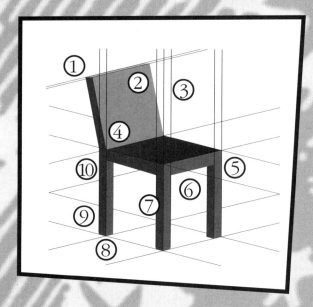

Step two

Choose each attribute one at a time and do something to it. Think of how your changes would affect the overall product.

Step three

Circle the three best ideas and write them out as a formal presentation. Show how they are workable and doable.

draw and quarter

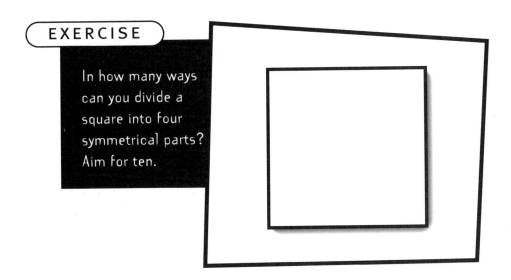

EXERCISE

In how many ways can you divide a square into four symmetrical parts? Aim for ten.

The purpose of analyzing a subject is to understand it better. Coming up with the most appropriate divisions sometimes takes a bit of trial and error.

My fourth-grade school teacher had a rule of thumb for approaching any new subject. The rule was to take the subject, divide it into four, and then divide each part into four again. For example, if you were studying law, you might think of:

The legal system

Lawyers

Law enforcement

Law reform

Under the legal system, you might think of criminal law, civil law, legislation and judges. Under lawyers, you might think of law schools, associations, in-house counsel and legal fees. Under law enforcement, you might consider police, surveillance, handcuffs and prison. And under law reform, you might think of politics, elections, equal rights legislation and tax laws.

The point is to use the number four as a quota for your new divisions. Four is a solid number and usually generates a satisfying collection of alternatives. So if you are confronted by the problem, "How can I improve my financial position?" divide the issue into four categories: savings, tax planning, cash management and investments. Further subdividing each portion will help you identify the areas that need work and will help you discover new ways of managing your finances.

The idea of dividing something into four has a psychological sense of completeness and is found in many
examples throughout history. Aristotle divided the universe into four elements — fire, earth, air and water.
Galen believed that human health was controlled by the
four humors — blood, phlegm, choler and black bile.
Psychologist Carl Jung arranged the human being into
four capacities: thinking, feeling, sensation and intuition.
And science — until quite recently — formulated the ele-
mentary forces of nature into electromagnetism, the
strong force, the weak force and gravity.

Consider a number of possible ways
to divide a square
into four parts.

There are many interesting ways of dividing a subject.
Sometimes though, a straightforward division can elude us. Look at the following two shapes divided into four pieces.

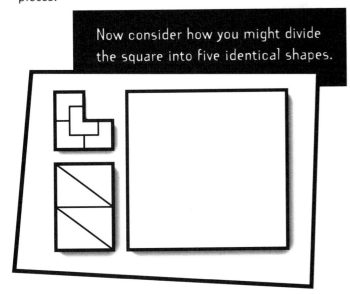

Now consider how you might divide the square into five identical shapes.

Often a solution gets blocked by preconceptions. The answer to the square problem is to divide the square into five parallel strips. Without the other figures, this answer is much easier to discover. But the two figures provide a misleading context, suggesting that square divisions must be complex shapes. I have seen people with Ph.Ds work at the problem for 20 minutes before seeing the solution.

Having fixed ways of categorizing and viewing a subject often limits how we relate to a subject. Often, the more familiar a person is with a subject, the more difficult it is to generate new ideas about it. Two researchers, Ellen Langer and Cynthia Weinman, conducted an experiment in Boston examining the ways in which unemployed people spoke about finding work. They asked people standing in an unemployment line to speak into a tape recorder for a "study of voice quality." Half the people were asked to talk about why it was difficult to find a job in Boston and the other half were asked to speak about getting a job in Alaska. These groups were further divided so that one half were given time to think of the answers before speaking, while the other half had to speak as soon as the question was posed.

The people who had time to think about getting a job in Alaska had the most ideas. People who had to immediately talk about getting a job in Boston also had many ideas. Meanwhile, the people who had lots of time to think about getting a job in Boston had fewer ideas, as did the people who had to answer spontaneously about finding work in Alaska.

This study suggests that we are most fluent when we have time to think about unfamiliar subjects and when we spontaneously express ideas about familiar subjects.

Conversely, we produce fewer ideas when we overanalyze familiar subjects. This suggests that there are two ways of generating new thoughts about familiar subjects. We can mentally step back and quickly rattle off as many ideas as we can — the basic intention of brainstorming. Or we can somehow make the subject unfamiliar.

examine the opposite

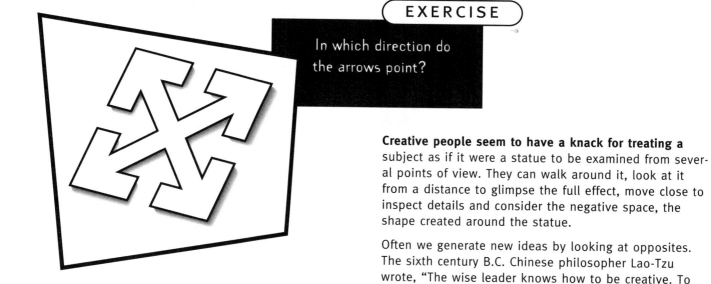

In which direction do the arrows point?

Creative people seem to have a knack for treating a subject as if it were a statue to be examined from several points of view. They can walk around it, look at it from a distance to glimpse the full effect, move close to inspect details and consider the negative space, the shape created around the statue.

Often we generate new ideas by looking at opposites. The sixth century B.C. Chinese philosopher Lao-Tzu wrote, "The wise leader knows how to be creative. To lead, the leader must learn to follow. To prosper, the leader must learn to live humbly. In both cases, it is the interaction which is creative."

Switching a mind-set to look at a subject's opposite does several things for our powers of analysis. We appreciate the feeling of relaxation more deeply after just having worked feverishly to reach a goal. And we know what we want as an outcome when we define what we don't want.

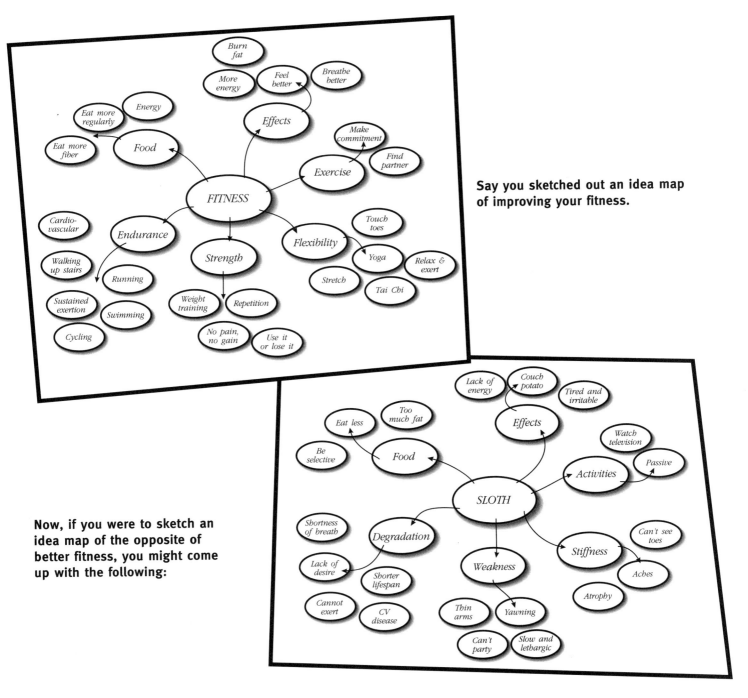

Say you sketched out an idea map of improving your fitness.

Now, if you were to sketch an idea map of the opposite of better fitness, you might come up with the following:

Exploring an idea through its opposite produces different trains of thought and can lead to different solutions. For example, rather than thinking of things to do to improve fitness, you may think of activities to avoid or stop doing.

Looking at the opposite can be refreshing. Look at the nearest piece of furniture, focus on the space surrounding it and you'll see in a new way. Look at the white space surrounding the text and photographs in a magazine and you'll attend to a key graphic design element. Think of opportunities surrounding problems to generate new perspectives. Look at a problem backward to discover a fresh idea.

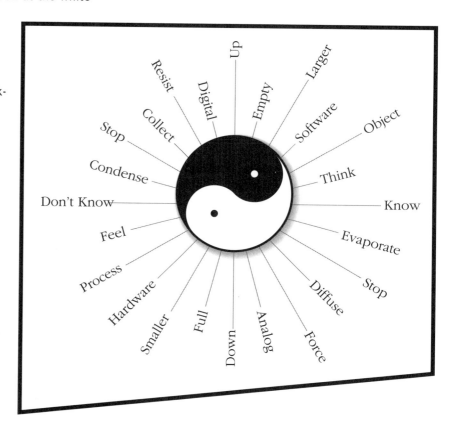

Businessman Ralph Stayer's company manufactures sausages. Once, at a time when the company was at risk of going under, Stayer took a close look at his products. He paid particular attention to how the company classified the sausages. All levels of employees, from senior management to factory workers, classified the sausages according to the way each was manufactured. In a moment of inspiration, Stayer asked what if the company reclassified the sausages according to how people ate them. Stayer looked at sausages in a number of new categories:

He asked questions such as, "What do people eat with their morning sausages?" Many people, he discovered, like to pour maple syrup on top of their breakfast weenies. The company started to manufacture and market a breakfast sausage with the maple syrup already added. Stayer found that some people like to eat sausages with beer, so he developed a beer-flavored sausage. Other sausages had Italian red wine flavors. Once the company had put their products into new categories, they could look at them in new ways. Stayer's ideas revitalized the sausage company. Before long, it enjoyed the highest market share, even while its products commanded the highest prices.

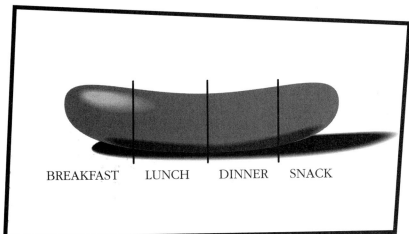

BREAKFAST   LUNCH   DINNER   SNACK

Children are masters when it comes to changing contexts. When I brought home a slide to my 18-month-old daughter, she knew just what to do with it. She climbed up and slid down. After a while she climbed underneath it and it became a bridge. She draped a blanket over it and made it into a house. She used it as a place to keep her stuffed toys. She placed her tea set on a step and used it as a table. Depending on the context, the slide served a different purpose.

One classic creative-thinking exercise is to invent as many uses as you can for an ordinary brick. A solid brick doesn't generally inspire revelations, but if you imagine the brick in different contexts or environments, suddenly a wealth of possibilities emerge. Try asking yourself how you could use the brick in your basement or in your bathroom.

Imagine uses the brick might have in an airplane, an art gallery, in a day-care center or in a glass factory. Go ahead and think of 20 possible uses for a brick.

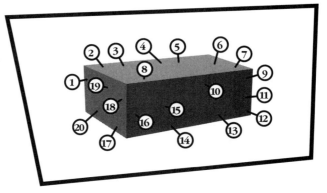

1

2 _____

3 _____

4 _____

5 _____

6 _____

7 _____

8 _____

9 _____

10 _____
_____

11 _____

12 _____

13 _____

14 _____

15 _____

16 _____

17 _____

18 _____

19 _____

20 _____

Often, the block to a creative solution to a problem is narrow focus within a single frame of reference. The person who can combine several frames of reference and discover the connections is more likely to produce the creative breakthrough.

With bricks you can build a house, construct a chimney, pave a walkway and stack the leftover bricks on the front yard and call it art. You could use a brick to pound on a neighbor's door, telling him to turn down the music or use it to kill his dog. You could crush the evidence and use it to make pigment and produce more art. You could use a brick as a doorstop, or to raise a pan in the oven. You can juggle bricks, smash them together to demonstrate particle physics or use the rough surface as a scrub pad. What else can you come up with?

Consider how a new context can transform a specialty product into something with universal appeal. In 1956, the Jacuzzi brothers, who sold water pumps to farmers, designed and built a whirlpool to treat their cousin's arthritis. Twelve years later, one of the brothers put the idea of the whirlpool bath into a new context — luxury baths — and bathrooms were never the same again.

Our sense of context and categories can become remarkably strong. Consider the Gregorian calendar. It's familiar, universally accepted and follows arbitrary rules. From 1793 to 1805, the French government adopted a new metric calendar which attempted to bring the units of time into harmony with each other. The metric year was divided into 12 months of 30 days. Each month was divided into three weeks of ten days — starting with seven days of work and ending with three days of rest. The days were given Latin names, *primedi* to *decadi*. The months were named after qualities of seasons. The rules of this metric calendar had a clear, logical structure which is missing from our Gregorian calendar. However, the conceptual shift to this superior system was too great. We will probably not enjoy a metric calendar for many years to come.

New categories can offer fresh insight into a problem and generate many new solutions. A consulting firm was recently hired to examine senior executive burnout. The executives didn't feel like they were having as much fun as they did earlier in life. Their busy schedules kept them hemmed in by deadlines and the pressing demands of work. One consultant asked the executives to list all the ways of having fun that they could think of. But she also asked them to divide their answers into four columns — activities that took less than five minutes; those of five minutes to half hour in duration; those that required half hour to half a day; and, finally, activities that needed more than half a day to be enjoyed.

What the executives discovered was that most of their fun activities fell into the half day or longer category. They weren't having fun because they didn't have time to do the things they associated with fun. The solution: the executives needed to change their focus and find activities they could enjoy in short periods of time. When they focused on mini-breaks, they found outlets where they saw none before.

The act of categorizing is such a basic part of the way

we deal with the world, that we hardly know that we are doing it. When you look at the following pattern, what do you see?

You probably see alternating rows of crosses and dashes. Few people initially see this pattern as a series of vertical columns of alternating crosses and dashes. When you do, you impose a new way of looking at the figure.

Dr. Edward de Bono, who coined the expression lateral thinking, suggests the way we perceive and group ideas profoundly affects the way we solve problems. The vertical thinker stops at the first perceived pattern and uses that pattern as a solution. The vertical thinker is usually limited to conventional solutions because the perception doesn't allow for other possibilities.

The lateral thinker, on the other hand, tries to perceive several patterns before trying to solve a problem. Creativity, by nature, requires a different interpretation, a desire on the part of would-be creators to see something new. The psychologist William James once said, "Genius in truth means little more than the faculty of perceiving in an unhabitual way."

change perspectives

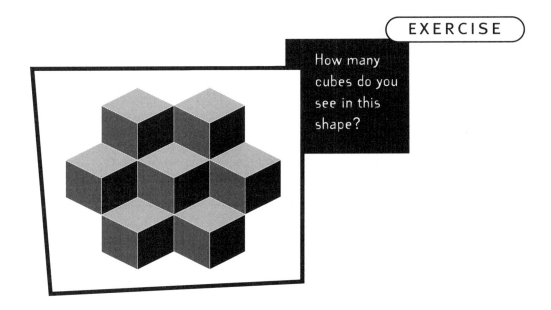

EXERCISE

How many cubes do you see in this shape?

Seeing familiar patterns in a new way often provides a fresh start to problem solving. A quick glance at the above shape shows seven cubes. Mentally flip your perspective so you view the cubes as if from below, rather than from above, and you see three cubes and parts of several others. The curious fact is that you can mentally change the orientation of the cubes at will. But nothing changes in the illustration — you only change your mind.

Flipping to a new point of view, or seeing something in a way which other people don't see, touches the essence of creative imagination. Something changes in your mind and you reframe what you see. You discover a new vantage point. These fresh discoveries often simplify complex problems.

It happened once that the mathematician Thomas Hardy walked past a colleague who was developing a puzzle for the Harvard mathematics competition. The problem was to prove that the tangent lines of any three circles will intersect on a point which lies on a straight line.

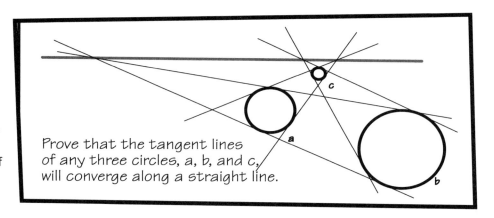

Prove that the tangent lines of any three circles, a, b, and c, will converge along a straight line.

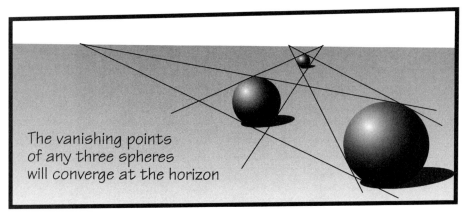

The vanishing points of any three spheres will converge at the horizon

Hardy looked at the puzzle for a moment and said, "Surely you must be joking. That problem is trivial. The proof is readily apparent without any further thought." His colleague, who thought the proof extraordinarily difficult, was astonished at Hardy's response.

What Hardy had done was turn the flat geometric construction into a three-dimensional picture. He viewed the three unequal circles as three equal spheres on a flat plane. The lines between the circles were lines of perspective. If you treat them as lying on a flat plane, then the perspective lines converge on the horizon. Remarkably, this relationship holds true in every case.

other people's viewpoints

How do we change perspectives? One good way is to imagine how another person might experience a subject. How would your grandmother see it? Your nephew? Your sixth-grade teacher? How would your dog — who is unable to understand any human language — view the situation? Really put yourself in their place.

To make the exercise more eclectic, put your thoughts on paper by sketching a series of idea maps. On one half of a page jot down their issues and concerns and on the other half sketch out yours. What fresh perspectives do you gain?

A friend of mine designs museum galleries. To evaluate her work she tours the gallery in an unusual way. First, she puts on dark sunglasses, walks through the gallery trying to read the signage, and asks, "How does a 70-year-old see this gallery?" Then she stops periodically, squats on the floor, looks around and asks, "How does a young child see this?" Then she ignores the signs completely and asks herself, "How does a foreign visitor see this gallery?"

The more perspectives you discover, the more likely you'll trigger something refreshing. In *Thunderbolt Thinking*, Grace McGarland plays with the idea of imagining you are the product. Thus, if you are a salesperson, imagine what a vacuum cleaner sees during a sales demonstration, what the car feels when the customer sits inside for the first time, how the books feel during shipping. What would it be like if you became the product for a whole afternoon? If you could see your product from the future or from the past, what would it look like? Move closer to focus on details. Move further away to see the big picture. There is no end to the choice of perspectives open to you.

Step one

List three people who are involved with the problem.

1. _____
2. _____
3. _____

Step two

Describe the problem from their points of view.

1. _____
   _____
   _____
2. _____
   _____
   _____
3. _____
   _____
   _____

Step three

Write down a suggestion from each of the people on how the problem should be solved.

1. _____
2. _____
3. _____

recipe for great ideas

**To sharpen your analytic powers,
try the following puzzles:**

Cube
How can you hold one cube so
that you can get another cube of
the same size to pass through
the first one?

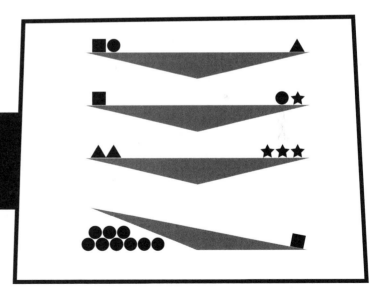

Balancing Act
How many circles would it take to balance
the square on the fourth set of scales?

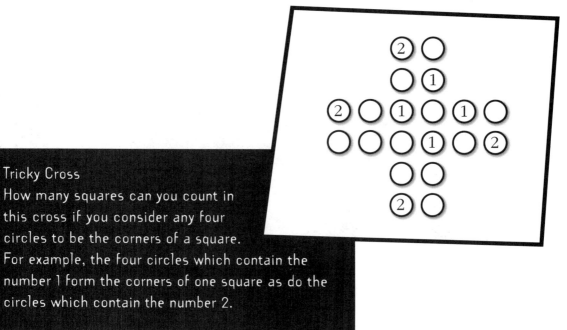

Tricky Cross

How many squares can you count in this cross if you consider any four circles to be the corners of a square. For example, the four circles which contain the number 1 form the corners of one square as do the circles which contain the number 2.

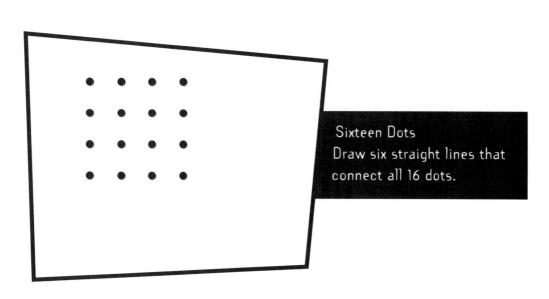

Sixteen Dots

Draw six straight lines that connect all 16 dots.

Tree Division
How can you divide this plot of land into four pieces of equal size with the same number of trees in each piece?

The Shortest Route
Connect all 12 houses by the shortest possible telephone cable. What is the shortest route that will carry you through all the houses? It can start at any house and does not need to return to its starting point.

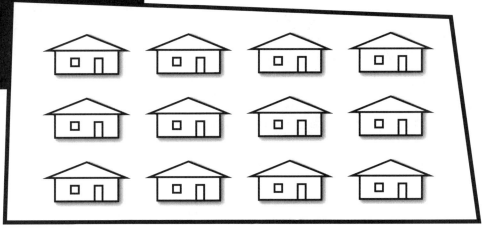

Unique Cube

How many ways is it possible to color the faces of a black cube white? Each way of coloring must produce a unique cube, one that cannot be turned into another by rotating it.

Simply Amazing

What is the simplest set of instructions you can give to go through the maze, from start to finish?

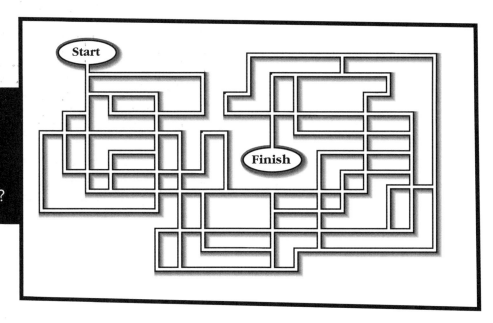

Tighter or Looser
When a metal washer is heated, does the hole increase in size, decrease in size or remain the same?

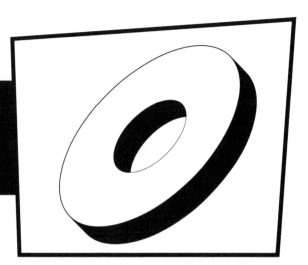

Connecting
Draw four paths connecting the like shapes. The paths may not cross or travel outside the square boundary.

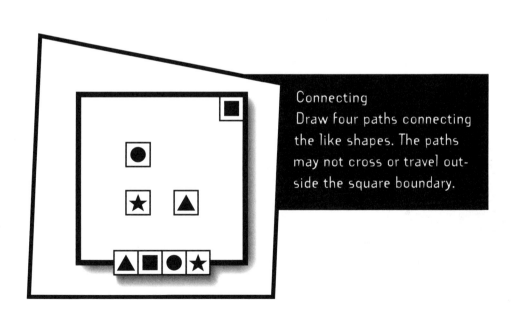

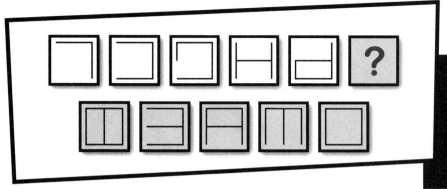

Visual Logic
Which shape from the
bottom row correctly
completes the sequence
in the top row?

Close Call
What are the thre mistake in this sentence?

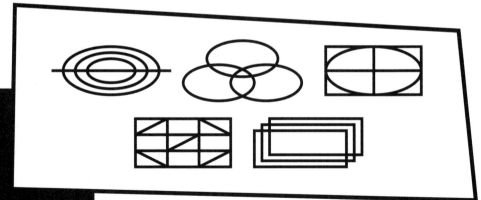

Single Strokes
Which of the following
five figures cannot be
drawn with a single
stroke without lifting
the pen off the paper or retracing?

94

Mental Analysis
How many possible routes are there from A to Z always traveling down or right? Can you work out the general rule relating the number of paths to the number of chambers?

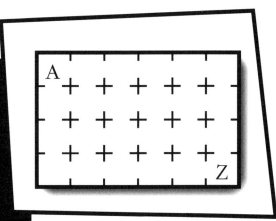

Behind the Scenes
How many cubes are in this symmetrical figure?

Squaring the Circle
How can you make two cuts in the following figure to produce a perfect square?

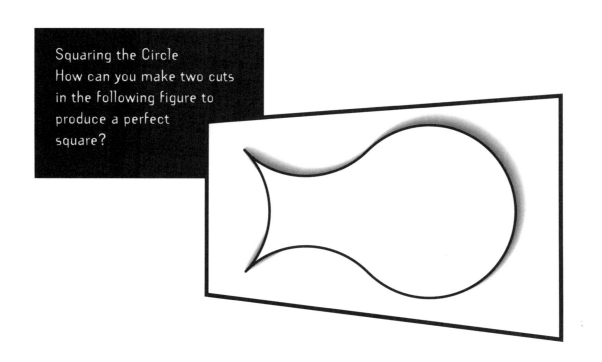

Creative Explanations
Exercise your ability to develop new explanations for situations and for natural phenomena by coming up with three fantastic explanations for the following events:

What causes disease?

Why is the sky blue?

Why are there stars?

Why does it snow?

WITNIIT...?

Figuring out patterns forms a large part of our intelligence. This skill helps us to determine similarities (people's facial features and accents), cycles (the phases of the moon), shapes (how to construct tools and building), processes (how to get a kite into the air and keep it there), and probabilities (the chances of being in a plane crash are far less than getting run over by a car in a big city). Discovering patterns, principles, rules, tendencies, likelihoods and relationships gives new information.

Finding a pattern translates into discovering some cause or tendency. The missing letter in the sequence is S. The letters are the first letters of each word for the question, "What is the next item in this sequence?"

Life is rarely ordered so clearly. The patterns we do discern are rich and more complex. Finding them is as rewarding and stimulating and keeps our mind sharp to life's details.

Junk mail

Scan your mail before you throw it out. What new trends in advertising, marketing, new products and values do you pick up? Let your junk mail accumulate for a month and see what happens.

Popular music

What are the trends in popular music? Is it getting louder or softer? More intimate or more intimidating? Is it more culturally diverse? Have the instruments changed? Do radio stations play more or less variety than five years ago?

Bookstores

Are there any consistent topics among best-sellers? What about magazine covers? What values does popular culture display? Who are the heroes and villains? Why are they portrayed as such?

Grocery stores

What are the new products? What products have disappeared or made a comeback? Which products have lasted? Are there new product categories?

Television shows

What are the trends in prime-time television? Is reality television becoming more or less popular? Are as many actors and actresses drifting over from movies into television? What kind of characters are portrayed on family shows now? Why are there plenty of shows about doctors, lawyers and police, and so few about scientists, politicians and engineers?

Television commercials

Are there new production techniques, or old ones which are being revived? What time of day are the best commercials on? The worst? Who is the intended audience for a particular commercial?

Clothing

Are hemlines going up or down? Are lapels getting wider or narrower? What are the fashionable colors this season? How do they compare with past seasons?

Everyday activities

Vilfredo Pareto, a nineteenth-century Italian economist, formulated a principle which we now call the 80-20 rule: 80 percent of a group's value can be found in 20 percent of the items in the group. For example, 80 percent of telephone calls come from 20 percent of your clients or friends. Eighty percent of ideas you remember come from 20 percent of what you read. Eighty percent of the traffic in an office occurs in 20 percent of the floor space. What are some other everyday patterns that show the 80-20 rule in action?

The search for patterns forces you to ask questions; and, as we saw in Chapter 2, questions help you unleash your creative powers.

mental maps

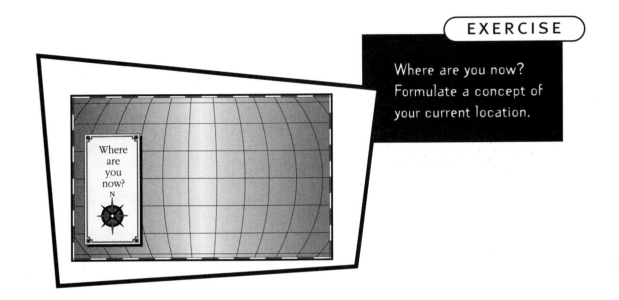

Where are you now?
N

What kind of map do you envision? You probably picture yourself in a room, which is located in a building, which exists as part of a network of streets and other buildings. You might even extend your mental map to include your city, country, continent, planet and galaxy.

The most familiar maps display geographic relationships. They illustrate distances, locations of landmarks and paths connecting various destinations. They are blueprints of reality.

Maps can adopt countless forms. A recipe is a map for cooking or baking. A script is a map for a movie. A family tree is a map of genetic interchange. A business plan is a map showing the path from a company's current condition to its desired state. Virtually any process can be mapped.

The Marshall Islanders developed stick charts before they acquired written language. Woven palm sticks, fastened with coconut fiber, represented hundreds of kilometers of open sea. Curved sticks symbolized prevailing wave fronts, shells pinpointed the position of islands and threads indicated where islands would come into view. The Inuit of Northern Canada carved rough sculptures representing bends in the coastlines. These maps — sturdy, functional and reliable — were carried on long canoe voyages on seal hunts.

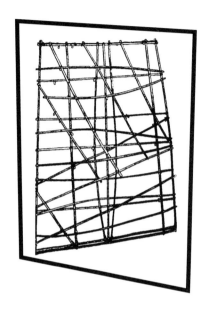

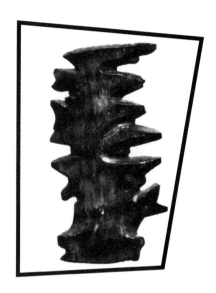

Marshall Islander's Map   **Eskimo Map**

Richard Saul Wurman, architect and designer writes,
"You cannot perceive anything without a map. A map
provides people with the means to share in the perceptions of others. It is a pattern made understandable; it
is a rigorous, accountable form that follows implicit principles, rules and measures." There are many maps we
can use to help develop and tease out ideas. The world
of business has its own maps to chart profit, loss and
market share, among other factors. Consider some other
ways of using maps:

The future map

Choose a subject, and surround it with the factors that
affect its future. This kind of map encourages you to
consider a wide range of data, such as taxes, consumer
tastes, interest rates, change in color preference and
lower manufacturing costs. Many trend-watch companies
use idea maps to generate maps of hundreds of publications and piece them together.

The team map

Encourage team participation by drawing a large idea map during brainstorming sessions. Because ideas don't initially have a hierarchy, and because every new idea fits into the existing map, the practice supports positive momentum. Consider leaving such a map in a staff room for a week.

The here-to-there map

Draw a starting map with two locations — here and there. Under "here," identify your current situation. It could be the state of a business relationship, your financial position or the status of a particular project. Then surrounding the world "there," list the factors which will characterize the ideal outcome. Next, work out the path from here to there. Say you wanted to be in Mongolia two weeks from today. What would you need to do to achieve your goal? Map out each step that you'd need to take, from getting a visa and hiring a guide — to buying a map!

The force field map

Life is like a pinball machine in which we are the ball, constantly subjected to forces trying to push and pull us in different directions. Understanding these forces helps to decide where your energy and resources are most effective. Put your idea in the center of a map. On one side list the factors which support your idea. These can

be time, opportunity, supportive people and so on. On this side describe the best-case scenario. On the other side of the map, list the factors which resist your idea, such as budget constraints, timing and the general mood of people involved. Then describe the worst-case scenario. Finally, look at the map and figure out what can be done to maximize the supporting factors and minimize the resisting factors.

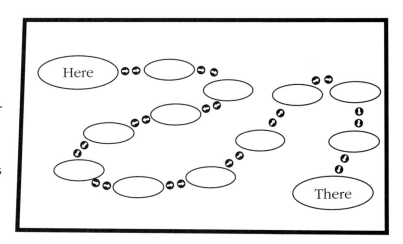

The context map

To better consider several points of view, create a map which includes you, your client and the two levels of management above and below you. Then write down a few sentences to illustrate each person's perspective. This map should help you find new relationships, connections and common factors. It should also help you identify the means of selling your idea to the people who matter, both inside and outside your company.

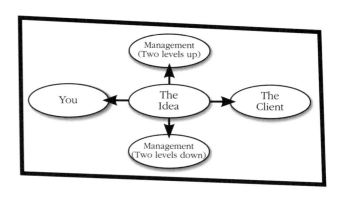

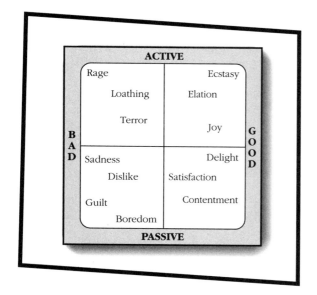

The idea grid map

Like other maps, idea grids compress large amounts of information into a single picture. Idea grids have many applications. Psychologist Charles Osgood, for example, used a grid to plot human emotions along two abstract qualities. In the following map, rage is active and bad, while boredom is bad and passive. This maps shows interesting connections between different emotions.

How might you plot emotions on the following grid? Which positive emotions make you feel like moving around? Which negative emotions compel you to remain still?

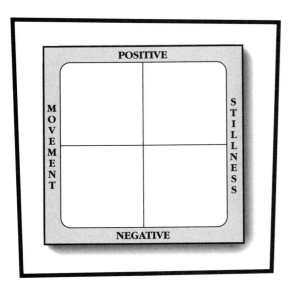

The Nippon Color and Design Institute uses idea grids to characterize business markets and to develop new niche products. The following map analyzes the perceived effect of women's pocket calculators. Note the three areas the company targeted for the calculator.

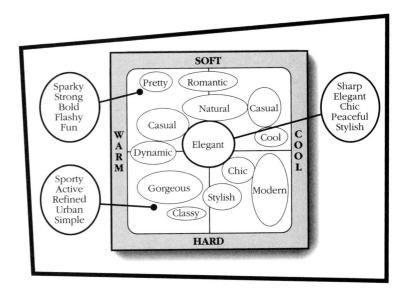

A grid can show new contexts and identify gaps in the market, predict the demand for new market ideas, assist in strategic planning and help you distance your firm from competitors. Consider a grid which sections off price and satisfaction. Where would a Honda Accord lie on this graph? A BMW? An Oldsmobile?

the six wise men

Six wise men of India
An elephant did find
And carefully they felt its shape
(For all of them were blind)

The first he felt toward the tusk,
"It does to me appear,
This marvel of an elephant
Is very like a spear."

The second sensed the creature's side
Extended flat and tall, "Aha!"
He cried and did conclude,
"This animal's a wall."

The third had reached toward a leg
And said, "It's clear to me
What we should all have instead
This creature's like a tree."

The fourth had come upon the trunk
Which he did seize and shake,
Quoth he, "This so-called elephant

Is really just a snake."
The fifth had felt the creature's ear
And fingers o'er it ran,
"I have the answer, never fear,
The creature's like a fan!"

The sixth had come upon the tail
As blindly he did grope,
"Let my conviction now prevail
This creature's like a rope."

And so these men of missing sight
Each argued loud and long.
Though each was partly in the right
They all were in the wrong.

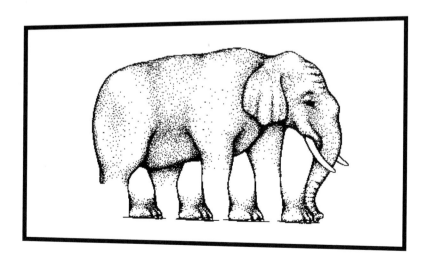

cutting

"THE CREATIVE PROCESS IS A MATTER OF CONTINUALLY
SEPARATING AND BRINGING TOGETHER,
BRINGING TOGETHER AND SEPARATING,
IN MANY DIMENSIONS — AFFECTIVE, CONCEPTUAL,
PERCEPTUAL, VOLITIONAL AND PHYSICAL."

ALBERT ROTHENBERG

Analysis is the act of clarifying information. Solving problems, defining objectives, determining causes, meaning and reasons all depend on crisp analysis. Cutting both simplifies information and adds to your knowledge of the subject.

Tip one

Break your problem or idea into its component parts. Study its attributes. If your subject is familiar, find ways of seeing it in a different light.

Tip two

Examine your idea from several points of view. Ask yourself, how will your customer see it? What will a six-year-old notice? What can a scientist get out of it? New perspectives provide new information and ideas. Avoid hardening of the categories.

Tip three

Arrange information visually. Use idea maps to keep track of facts, relationships and details — and to keep the information manageable.

mix

combine ideas

5

the aha principle

**Look at these letters, and rearrange them
until you discover a recognizable word.
Mix them freely. What do you find?**

the mixing bowl of ideas

"NEITHER THE POET'S WORDS
NOR THE INVENTOR'S THINGS
HAVE ANY REMARKABLE
PROPERTIES OF THEIR OWN.
THEY ARE EVERYDAY
WORDS AND THINGS.
IT IS THE JUXTAPOSITION
OF THEM WHICH IS NEW."

David Pye, Author

Each part of the creative-cooking process leads us along a route of generating fresh ideas: cultivating an appetite generates interest and passion, thereby stimulating our imagination; in gathering, we collect the raw ingredients to include in our stew; cutting encourages us to define and arrange information and to examine it from different perspectives. Mixing — the next step in the creative process — is another common culinary activity. In mixing we combine and blend ingredients to create something new and satisfying.

Mixing is what we do when we connect two or more items to produce a novel combination. The graphic designer who joins unrelated images to devise a corporate logo is involved in creative mixing. So is the product designer who marries the two ideas of plush toys and fuzzy slippers. The act of mixing has produced creations as revolutionary as Gutenburg's printing press (the grape press and the coin punch), as common as Band-Aids (gauze pads and surgical tape), and as remarkable as chaos theory (swirls of cream within coffee and the swirls of stars in spiral galaxies).

Discovering connections between apparently unrelated subjects lies at the heart of mixing ideas. Our minds constantly link different kinds of information. We busily combine memories, new information, aspirations, fears, intentions and objectives to produce new views of the world. It should be no surprise that the Latin word for thinking, *cogito* is derived from the root words *cum* and *agitare*, which means to shake together.

In this chapter we will explore a variety of ways of combining ideas. We will mix ideas by brute force, shaking them together and studying what comes out. We will look for good ideas by connecting a subject to an inanimate object, by using an idea matrix and by exploring the world of metaphor. But first, let's take a close look at the creative mind's ultimate stimulant — the moment of discovery.

the creative spark

Rearrange these six matches to produce four identical equilateral triangles.

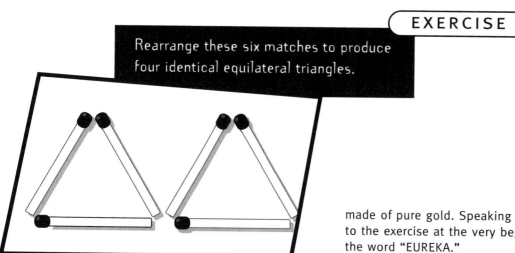

Probably the most quoted story of inspired discovery is that of the Greek philosopher, Archimedes. In the third century B.C., Archimedes was asked by his cousin, King Hieron II, to work out whether the royal crown was made of pure gold or of a mixture of gold and cheaper metals. Knowing that he couldn't melt or alter the crown, Archimedes pondered the problem for several weeks. One day, during a visit to the public baths, he lowered himself into the bath water, the water overflowed the tub — and the solution appeared in a flash. Archimedes could measure the crown's volume by submerging it in water. He could then compare that volume with a similar amount of real gold. Archimedes was so excited by his discovery, he ran naked through the streets shouting, "Eureka! I have found it!" Subsequently, he discovered that the crown was not

made of pure gold. Speaking of connections, the answer to the exercise at the very beginning of this chapter is the word "EUREKA."

Many people believe that a "eureka" belongs exclusively to big "C" creative experiences, and that genuine moments of discovery are always accompanied by dramatic emotional realizations. However, each of us experiences a series of "ahas" — smaller eurekas — throughout the day in little events.

daily eurekas

Kid's Joke
Why do cows wear bells?
Because their horns don't work!!

Children enjoy streams of daily "ahas" and "eurekas." Watch a first-grade class of students tour a zoo or a museum and you will see them making endless discoveries. We, as adults, can experience more "eurekas" by making ourselves more aware of the creative episodes we enjoy everyday. And that's not a bad thing to do: to be drawn to experiences which make us laugh more, appreciate beauty and pursue insight.

Have you solved the six-match problem? If you haven't, here's a hint: close your eyes and think in three dimensions. Can you make a three-dimensional structure which will meet the objective?

One of my favorite stories of creative connections comes from the childhood of R. Buckminster Fuller. His first-grade teacher instructed the class to construct model buildings out of toothpicks and dried peas. While other students built familiar objects such as houses, barns and stores, Fuller — who had poor eyesight — began to build shapes based on the way they felt, not how they looked. He liked triangles because they felt "stable, reliable and solid." In a short while, he constructed elaborate latticeworks, scaffolds and triangular structures many times larger than the ones made by the other students. Buckminster Fuller said, "I began to feel then that all nature's structuring and patterning must be based on triangles."

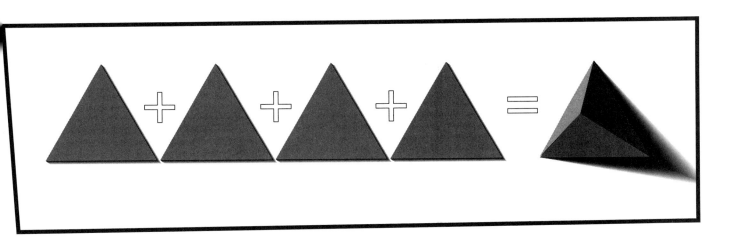

Two decades later, Fuller developed the geodesic dome, a structure which is remarkably stable, has no internal supports, and can enclose almost unlimited spaces. Today, there are over 300,000 geodesic domes and they can be found on every continent. Each dome is a practical, transportable and economical structure, based on a collection of the simplest of geometric shapes — the triangle. Buckminster Fuller's childhood discovery that solid three-dimensional shapes can be produced from two-dimensional triangles had a permanent effect on his approach to architecture, science and philosophy.

The solution to the six-match problem is to produce a tetrahedron. When you get the solution, a quick spark of insight lights up your intellect. This magical feeling is probably the most talked-about and least-understood part of creativity.

We hear that inspiration is a wild, uncontrolled energy of the creative mind. It is a sudden flash which produces the birth of a new idea. In some ways inspiration is involuntary. We will ourselves to have insight as we can will ourselves to concentrate. But if inspiration were wholly involuntary, we wouldn't be entitled to take credit for our ideas — only for our actions.

In fact, leaps of imagination come to those who prepare their minds and who make the effort to search. The French mathematician, Jules Henri Poincare wrote, "These sudden inspirations...never happen except after some days of voluntary effort which has appeared absolutely fruitless and whence nothing good seems to have come, where the way taken seems totally astray. These efforts then have not been as sterile as one

thinks; they have set agoing the unconscious machine, and without them it would not have moved and would have produced nothing."

So, famous stories of inspiration — the apple falling on Isaac Newton's head, Samuel Taylor Coleridge's epic poem, *Kubla Khan*, coming to him in a single dream, and Archimedes' insight into specific gravity — are heartening, but may be misleading. They understate the introspection that precedes the revelation. Searching, analyzing and connecting prepares the mind for insight. If you cut short the floundering, you reduce the possible creative outcomes. If you avoid the chaotic stumbling about, you rob yourself of the raw stuff that feeds your imagination.

Step one

Prepare yourself for inspiration. Adopt a mind-set of discovery by highlighting the subject at hand. Deeply immerse yourself in the study of your subject. Give yourself enough time to walk around the idea, examining it from different perspectives.

Step two

Look around for fresh ideas you can connect to your subject. McArthur Fellowship winner and stage director Peter Sellars searches for artistic interpretation in the most unlikely places. He combines martial arts with deaf signing, rock videos with myth, traditional opera with modern situations. The lead character in Mozart's *Don Giovanni* eats Big Macs and uses a switchblade instead of a sword. Handel is set in a Middle East crisis and King Lear drives a Lincoln Continental. Sellars's interpretations meet mixed reactions, but each performance brings brand new interpretations and shakes up traditional theatrical ideas.

Step three

Make mental connections. Say you wanted to write the text for a greeting card which has a picture of an apple on the front. How would you generate ideas? You could link an apple to the words red, shiny, pie, round, crunchy, organic, computer, records, seed and tree. You might connect it to cider, corer, teacher, sauce, William Tell, George Washington and Isaac Newton. The more lively your internal dialogue, the more ideas will come to you and the more your creative energy level will rise. And as it rises, you tap into the satisfying sensation of successive eurekas.

the idea mixmaster

Can you see a triangle in the following figure?

Our minds constantly fill in shapes and patterns based on our expectations. Even where there is no triangle in the figure — just three circles with a slice cut out of them — our brain fills one in.

A connection is a link between objects that can be based on similarities as well as differences. Our minds easily connect chair and table, ham and eggs, brother and sister, work and money and so on. And this ability to find connections is one of our mightiest creative assets; we can use it in many ways to generate creative energy.

An elementary-school friend of mine once told me that he could connect anything to peanut butter. You might

say "cup," and he would say "Well, a cup holds the milk that you drink while you eat a peanut butter sandwich." If you said, "wheat fields," he would say "Of course peanuts and wheat are closely related genetically. And they're almost the same color." You might say, "The Andromeda Galaxy," and he would say "Both have swirls!" These connections might have been tenuous but he never missed a beat.

Finding connections through free association works with all kinds of ideas. Freewheeling propels us toward inspiration. As you make spontaneous connections you generate ideas which will lead to real solutions and real products.

A quick look in any kitchen shows plenty of ways people have joined unrelated objects to create a brand new product. Ziploc food-storage bags borrow the idea of a zipper and impose it onto plastic. The tube container for Pillsburry crescent rolls was developed in a brainstorming session, borrowing an idea from pea pods. A Teflon-coated iron borrows its technology from no-stick frying pans.

A farmer from Brandon, Manitoba connected trading cards with farm animals and came up with bovine trading cards.

The cards, depicting the finest show-quality cows in Canada and the United States, include photographs, statistics of the cows' backgrounds and breeding potential. Buyers — and there are many — like the cards' educational value, not to mention their kitsch appeal.

For fun and practice, think of five different ways you can combine a chair and a wheel to produce something new.

Chair + Wheel = ?

In 1893, George Washington Gale Ferris Jr. combined the two to produce the world's first "Pleasure Wheel" in Chicago. You might conceive of a wheelchair, a baby chair with a play steering wheel, several chairs on the edge of a large horizontal wheel in a children's theme restaurant or a window-washer seat which is raised and lowered by a large flywheel. Now see if you can come up with more combinations. Vary the size and relationships until you've got five more ideas.

Here are some more pairings you can use to practice producing connections.

Button and Stove

Telescope and Shovel

Ear and Fire

Film and Piano

Ball and Raft

Table and Lever

Wave and Sex

God and Kaleidoscope

random words

EXERCISE

You are chairing a committee on water conservation and management. You flip through a dictionary and randomly point to a word. Think up six ideas about water management based on the following word:

JAIL

When you search for connections between a word and a specific problem, you'll find any number of useful associations. Imagine listening in on the inner dialogue of someone working through the problem.

"Water and jail. Let's see, hmmm. Water leaks through the bars of a jail cell. So what are the equivalent bars in the water system? If we can isolate them, we'll be able to close some of them off. Jail. We could hand down real jail sentences to people who waste water. We could keep people in their homes as a kind of jail sentence and limit their water supply. Let's see, what else? What's a jail? A jail holds people. Jails are holding tanks. Perhaps we can build better holding tanks to

116

store the water. Jails have small cells. Maybe we can better distribute water into many water cells. Each home could have water cells, which are filled on a monthly basis. This will be their allocated water for the month. Or, we could run a public campaign using household water meters. Each month we'd send families a report on their water consumption showing the total visually — say, as the equivalent of so many bathtubs or swimming pools. This campaign could include little stickers to remind people to conserve water — while brushing teeth, taking showers and so on. Jail. Hmm. Jail and water. Ice is locked up water. There's that idea to float icebergs from Alaska to California and melt them into drinking water. How else can we unlock water? From air. Look at the technology of getting drinking water from moisture in air. Is this realistic? Jail. Jails are dungeons and dungeons are often deep in the ground. How else can we dig for ground water?"

The more you connect, the more you find. You can select random words from any source. Dictionaries, thesauruses, encyclopedias, magazines, quote books, all make great raw ingredients for stews.

Writer and teacher Natalie Goldberg suggests how to let your mind fool around freely by making up new connections. When you want to tap into creative energy while writing, take three or four lines of your text and write them at the top of a piece of paper. Then view each word as a wooden block, all the same size, shape and color. No word — noun, verb, adjective or conjunction — has greater value than any other.

Take about a third of these words and start jumbling them around. Don't try to make sense of what you write down. Your brain will attempt to construct something and make logical sense and structure. Hold back that urge. Just relax and mindlessly write down the words. Write over and over until you've filled the page.

Add a few periods, some commas and one or two question and exclamation marks. Do it for fun, without thinking about it. Breaking out from the subject/verb/object pattern makes you see the world in new ways.

If you write at a word processor, turn off the computer monitor and just type ideas in as fast as you can. Don't look back. Don't stop to check for spelling. Just let your words come freely.

**Use random words to generate a fresh approach.
The best words are those which are simple, visual
and full of associations.**

Step one

Write down your opening question:
"In what ways can I _____?"

Step two

Choose a random word from the list on the following page or from
any other source, such as a magazine, dictionary, thesaurus, radio or
television show.

Step three

Look for connections between the word and your problem. Are there
similarities or differences? Listen to the sound of the word. Find figurative
links. Consider the characteristics of both.

Step four

Establish an idea quota and give yourself enough time to fully explore the
possibilities. To keep your ideas from slipping away, make sure you record
them on a sheet of paper or in your idea journal. Store the results for
future consideration.

random word list

Lamp	Computer	**Vacuum**	Poker	**Weed**	Toilet
Cotton	Radio	**Hammer**	Scabbard	**Handcuffs**	Circle
Pants	Ring	**Palm**	Finger	**Bail**	Coil
Pencil	Engine	**Soul**	Chocolate	**Recital**	Rope
Television	Food	**Ticket**	Funeral	**Nut**	Hose
Tree	Slogan	**Operation**	Single	**Flavor**	Disease
Cigarette	Marvel	**Cell**	Stopwatch	**Sink**	Stretch
Plantation	Rock	**Lens**	Bingo	**Tape**	Army
Knife	Judge	**Avalanche**	Child	**Rifle**	Backbone
Starfield	Train	**Ride**	Bomb	**Bamboo**	Vessel
Book	Mountain	**Rope**	Speedboat	**Halloween**	Socks
Telephone	Game	**Screw**	Bear	**Forgery**	File
Camera	Fan	**Disk**	Cathedral	**Weight**	Chair
Dictionary	Sewer	**Hourglass**	Factory	**Symbol**	Marble
Ladder	Scrape	**Flash**	Rum	**Ink**	Dinner
Contract	Concert	**Carpet**	Baseball	**Copy**	Shell
Moon	Jail	**Cave**	Pendulum	**Face**	Code
Microscope	Cross	**Chill**	Skin	**Square**	Cloud
Issue	Joke	**Bed**	Safe	**Bedroom**	Glow
Motor	Disco	**Piano**	Moccasin	**Handle**	Strap
Brain	Religion	**Door**	Blender	**Fold**	Sauce
Jewelry	Closet	**Spider**	Race	**Catapult**	Fire

object linking

Another way to get your creative juices flowing is to choose a familiar object such as a pencil, hold it in your hands and use it as a source of inspiration. Consider how an ordinary wooden pencil can lead you to new ideas about advancing your career:

How could you link your idea with a book, keyboard, watch, coin, iron, teapot or telephone?

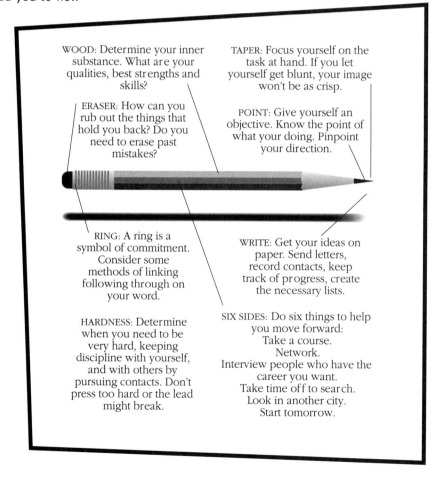

WOOD: Determine your inner substance. What are your qualities, best strengths and skills?

TAPER: Focus yourself on the task at hand. If you let yourself get blunt, your image won't be as crisp.

ERASER: How can you rub out the things that hold you back? Do you need to erase past mistakes?

POINT: Give yourself an objective. Know the point of what your doing. Pinpoint your direction.

RING: A ring is a symbol of commitment. Consider some methods of linking following through on your word.

WRITE: Get your ideas on paper. Send letters, record contacts, keep track of progress, create the necessary lists.

HARDNESS: Determine when you need to be very hard, keeping discipline with yourself, and with others by pursuing contacts. Don't press too hard or the lead might break.

SIX SIDES: Do six things to help you move forward:
Take a course.
Network.
Interview people who have the career you want.
Take time off to search.
Look in another city.
Start tomorrow.

mental hieroglyphics

Professor Michael Ray of the Stanford University School
of Business gets his students' minds moving by having
them link a business venture with Egyptian hieroglyph-
ics. The patterns are rich with meaning and set the mind
moving. For example, imagine that you are planning to
make a fortune in real estate. Look at the following
shapes and figures and make up a story which will help
you plan your way.

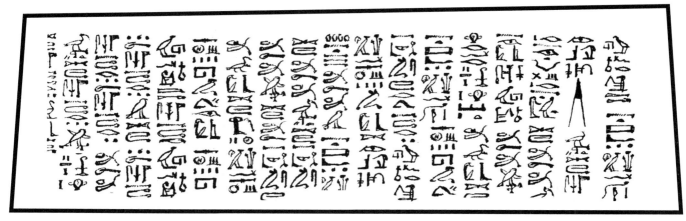

Each figure in this selection from the *Egyptian Book of
the Dead* can be used to generate several meanings.
The birds can become vultures (real-estate agents) or
symbols of freedom (capital investors). The figures of
people can represent home renovators or clients. The
wave pattern may represent assets or liabilities.
Imagine how you might interpret these shapes if you
were thinking about writing a mystery novel, starting a
frozen yogurt business or making up an ad
campaign for a new soup.

make variations

Rearrange five buttons so that each button touches every other button.

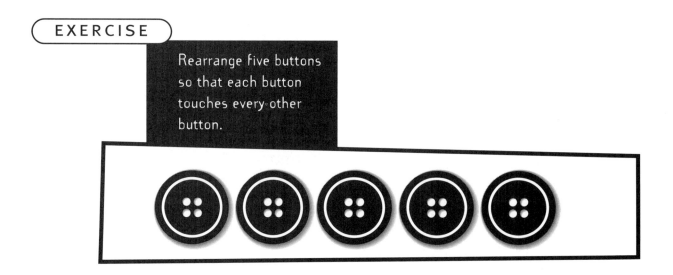

In 1901, the inventor Hubert Cecil Booth visited an exhibition of innovations at a London music hall. An American inventor (whose name is lost to history) showed a wonderful machine for removing dust from carpets. The machine blew air — and made everyone in the first six rows sneeze. After the demonstration, Booth went to see the man and suggested that the machine should suck, not blow. The man responded, "Suck? Suck? Sucking is not possible!" and stormed out of the room. Booth later was credited for the invention of the vacuum cleaner.

Inventors and innovators often build on the work of those who have gone before. Consider the development of the telescope. In 1609, Hans Lippershey, a Danish eyeglass maker, held two lenses in front of each other and discovered that they magnified (and inverted) the image. By 1659, Johannes Hevelius lengthened the telescope to 150 feet to get a larger image and to prevent chromatic aberration — the scattering of light in a rainbow of colors. A few years later, Robert Hooke shortened the telescope tube by using flat mirrors to reflect the light back and forth several times. In 1668, Isaac Newton constructed a telescope which gathered light with a curved mirror rather than with a lens. A French sculptor, Monsieur Cassegrain improved on the Newtonian design by using two curved mirrors. These yielded a sharper focus while requiring a smaller tube.

When the 200-inch glass slab for the Palomar observatory was first cast, the glass cracked. To help cool the mirror, the builders scooped out excess glass from the back (which also made the mirror lighter). Modern research telescopes now use combinations of mirrors as well as thin, flexible mirrors which are continually monitored and adjusted by computers.

If, at times, your imagination is as blank as an empty stare, take an existing item and manipulate it.

Remember that everything new is just an addition or modification to something that preceded it. You just need time to come up with a variation that satisfies the objective.

Say you wanted to improve the design of a telephone. Choose three verbs from the following list and mentally apply that action to the telephone. What do you get?

Add	Darken	**Cycle**	Extract	**Seduce**
Subtract	Complement	**Defend**	Dither	**Glue**
Extrude	Freeze	**Vibrate**	Define	**Colorize**
Pull	Unify	**Shift**	Distort	**Multiply**
Repel	Dissect	**Loosen**	Copy	**Divide**
Protect	Magnify	**Hatch**	Coerce	**Invert**
Segregate	Compress	**Skid**	Bury	**Transpose**
Integrate	Squeeze	**Return**	Concentrate	**Separate**
Symbolize	Wring	**Broaden**	Mash	**Flatten**
Abstract	Drop	**Stalk**	Mince	**Rotate**
Stretch	Display	**Crack**	Connect	**Fluff up**
Thicken	Eliminate	**Harden**	Continue	
Brighten	Force	**Blur**	Insert	

mixing puzzles

Brainteasers are to your mind as stretching is to your body. Both develop flexibility. Most of the following teasers are "aha" puzzles: they can be bewildering until you look at them in a new way. If you persevere by loosening your mind and trying new approaches, you'll experience that electric "aha" sensation when you solve it.

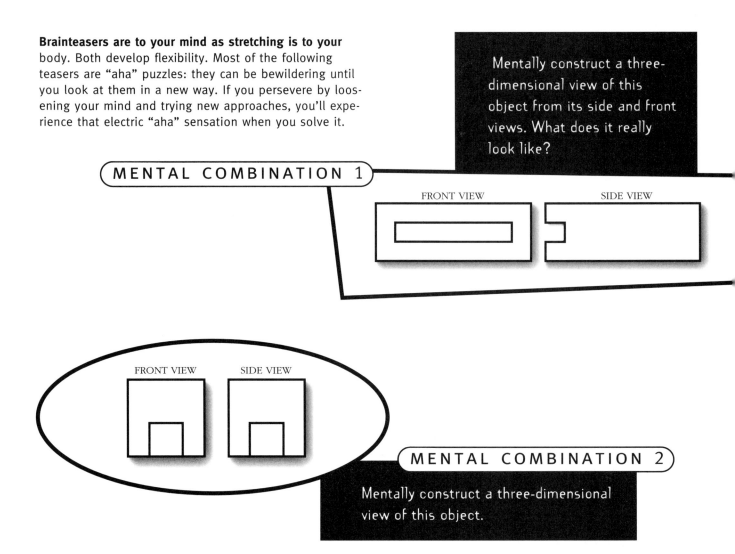

Mentally construct a three-dimensional view of this object from its side and front views. What does it really look like?

MENTAL COMBINATION 1

FRONT VIEW   SIDE VIEW

FRONT VIEW   SIDE VIEW

MENTAL COMBINATION 2

Mentally construct a three-dimensional view of this object.

Mental Gymnastics

A glass is filled one third with wine. A second glass is filled one quarter with wine. Water is added to the top of each glass. Half of each glass is poured out, then the remaining liquid is combined in one glass. What portion of the final mixture is wine?

Ten people are sitting at a table. During the toast, each person clinks his or her glass with every other person. How many separate clinks would you hear? Can you determine a general rule linking the number of clinks to the number of glasses?

RUBBER SQUARES

One of the square figures can be stretched into the circle figure. Which is it?

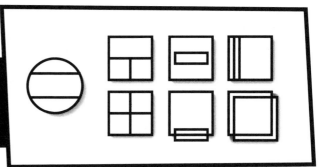

Can you arrange these nine dots into nine rows of three dots each?

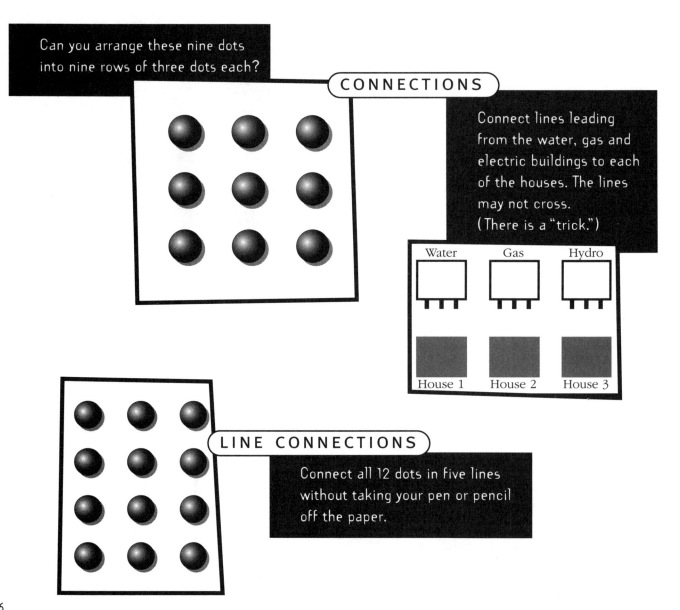

CONNECTIONS

Connect lines leading from the water, gas and electric buildings to each of the houses. The lines may not cross.
(There is a "trick.")

Water | Gas | Hydro

House 1 | House 2 | House 3

LINE CONNECTIONS

Connect all 12 dots in five lines without taking your pen or pencil off the paper.

MATCH PUZZLES

The collection of 24 matchsticks form a three by three grid. Mentally rearrange the matches to achieve the following objectives:

Obtain five identical squares by removing four sticks.

Obtain five identical squares by removing six sticks.

Obtain three squares by removing eight sticks.

Obtain four identical squares by removing eight sticks.

Obtain two squares by removing eight sticks.

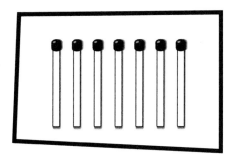

Intimate Contact

Can you rearrange seven matchsticks so that every match touches every other match?

Four Rows

Can you rearrange two buttons to create two rows with four buttons in each row?

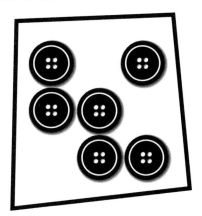

lateral-thinking puzzles

Lateral-thinking puzzles challenge your powers of questioning and deduction. To solve them you need to approach them from the side; inspiration strikes when you look at them in a "different" way.

When an employee took over the job of sorting and delivering our corporate mail for two weeks, the mail was no longer tossed haphazardly into the bins. Instead, it was neatly arranged in the center of each bin and each bundle had an elastic band around it. I asked the person why he did this. He said, "Well, it may seem that I am doing more work, but actually I'm saving myself from more work. Normally two or three people from each department walk into the mail room each day. They sort through the piles and take their own personal mail leaving the rest of the department's. It turns out that when the mail is in a neat bundle, they almost always take the whole bundle back to the department, saving me a delivery trip."

The Amazing Shrinking Cup

Take an ordinary coffee cup and a square piece of paper, say eight inches by eight inches, and cut a one-inch circular hole through the paper. Can you push a coffee cup through the hole?

Missing Bears

The young patients at a children's hospital loved to play with the cuddly teddy bears so much that the children would take them home. How did the hospital solve the problem? The hospital did not lock up the bears, make the bears unattractive or penalize the children.

New Word

What common word starts with "IS", ends with "ND" and has "LA" in the middle?

Use these questions to find new ways of mixing and matching.

What can you modify?

Can you alter a current process or system? What procedures can you add, eliminate or replace? Does someone else have an approach that would work better than the one you use?

What can you substitute?

Substitution is a trial-and-error method of reaching your goal. Thomas Edison substituted 1,700 materials before finding the right filament for a light bulb. What can be substituted? Who can be replaced? Can the rules be changed? The ingredients? Procedures?

What can you combine?

Are there new combinations of ideas, ingredients or techniques which will serve you better? Can combining elements improve your efficiency?

What can you adapt?

What else is like this? What other idea does this suggest? Does the past offer a parallel? What other process could be adapted? Do other contexts or industries suggest ideas you can incorporate?

What can you magnify?

What can be magnified or extended? What can be exaggerated? Can you go further, higher or faster? Can you add new features? Create greater value?

What can you eliminate or minify?

What if it were smaller? What can you omit? What can you streamline, condense or compact? What is unnecessary?

What use can you change?

What else can this be used for? Are there new ways to use it as is?

What can you rearrange?

A baseball manager has 362,880 ways of shuffling his lineup. What can you rearrange? Consider staffing, layouts, blueprints, systems, scheduling and priorities.

the idea matrix

How quickly can you fill in the remaining squares by combining the shapes across the top row with the shapes down the first column?

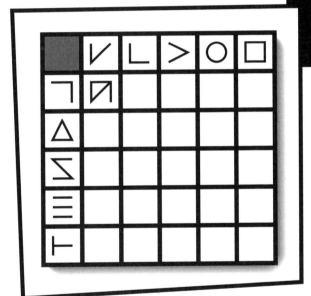

A road map mileage chart shows the distance between various locations. Similarly, an idea matrix shows relationships between different objects or concepts. The items can be anything which will help you generate ideas. For example, if you wanted to produce an idea matrix for a new child's toy, you might start by listing attributes of toys. Toys can bounce, fall, spin, stack and fit into each other. Put these items across the top of a chart. Now think of some other qualities of toys. Toys can be round, square, soft, furry and colorful. List these items down the side of the chart. Finally, combine the concepts and see what you get. Your first ideas may not be brilliant. But you will get ideas that you wouldn't have arrived at in other ways. Concepts may include soft toys that roll, square toys that spin and furry, stackable toys. Look for combinations which capture your imagination.

Idea matrices can be applied to almost any circumstance. Fashion designers can use them to produce variations of clothing, combining, say, different kinds of collars — round, V-neck, scoop neck, mandarin — with types of sleeves — draped, tapered, short and puffed. Furniture designers can use them to combine materials — wood, metal, cloth and plastic with different bases — wheels, swivel, tilt, three-legged and beanbag. Consultants can use idea matrices to generate new options combining their objectives — to live in the country, work from home, feel creative — with their skills — proficiency with computers, ability to write quickly and ability to make excellent presentations. Consider the following matrix and the different combinations it yields.

	SKILLS				
	Computer skills	Interest in nature	Stimulate children	Public speaking	Well organized
Live in country					
Work at home					
Creative work					
Time for family					
Write articles		●			

OBJECTIVES

Write articles about nature

make metaphors

Metaphors — and their relatives, similes, analogies, parallels, allegories, symbols, allusions — are much more than figures of speech. They are the architects of our conceptual system; they build scaffolds of ideas. We usually think of a metaphor as a statement which expresses one concept in terms of another. Consider the notion popularized by Benjamin Franklin:

If we *conceive* of time as a commodity, then we *act* as if it were a valuable, yet limited, resource. Time becomes a substance which can be spent, wasted, invested, saved, managed. We become upset at the loss of time. The metaphor, "time is money," provides us with a complete conceptual strategy for dealing with daily time.

Of course, time is not money, really. Time, once spent, cannot be returned. You cannot save time in a bank, nor can you accumulate interest. Time is not a tangible object which can be handled, like coins and currency.

Other metaphors of time provide different conceptual frameworks. Time can be a river, carrying us along. If time is a landscape, then life is a mix of uncluttered vistas of free time and busy forests of activity. If time is a castle, then traveling through time is like moving through a collection of connected yet separate rooms, a symbol of the partitions of our daily routines. Each metaphor provides a new perspective, a

TIME IS MONEY

"She is *wasting* my time."

"I can't *afford* to lose any more time."

"Is that *worth* your time?"

"Can you *set aside* some time for swimming?"

"A daytimer can help you *budget* your time more effectively."

"He can't *give* you any *more* time."

"Have you been *spending* your time wisely?"

"If you don't *use* your time more profitably, you will *run out* of it sooner than you think."

new set of associations and fresh creative tension and energy. Consider how switching metaphors gives us new ways of examining an idea:

Ideas are food

They swallowed his half-baked notions. I'm just beginning to digest what he said. That's a theory you can sink your teeth into. I am just beginning to stew over those ideas. Those chapters are the meaty part of the book.

Ideas are products

The group is churning out plenty of ideas, and will soon smooth out the rough edges. The other company can't produce any successful ideas. Our creative director knows the secret of refining ideas.

Ideas are people

Those ideas, which gave birth to modern physics, breathed life into the university. Artificial intelligence is still in its infancy. Those notions died off and were replaced with others which will live for a long time.

Ideas are plants

He planted the theory into the budding minds of his students. Eventually it came to full flower in their fertile imaginations. Those ideas are in the germinal phase. Her thoughts finally came to fruition. Physics has many branches and offshoots.

Ideas are resources

Finally, he exhausted his ideas, but the ones that he mined will go a long way. She knows how to dig deep for new information. If she learns to package her ideas better, they will be more useful.

Ideas are light sources

Your presentation highlighted the problems, and brilliantly showed the whole picture. The discussion was illuminating. The new refinements are dazzling, and reflect well on the company.

How easily we adopt different conceptual frameworks! We think of love as a force (There were sparks), love as a battle (I made advances), love as madness (I'm crazy about her) or love as magic (They are spellbound by each other). We think of arguments as war (I launched my attack), arguments as buildings (We are constructing a strong foundation), arguments as journeys (He still hasn't covered much ground) and arguments as containers (He has put all the facts into his presentation). We think of learning as acquiring (He is gathering knowledge), learning as vision (His intellect sees features others miss) and learning as exploring (That child is constantly making discoveries).

Eric Donald Hirsch Jr., author of the *Dictionary of Cultural Literacy*, stresses the importance of linking old and new ideas: "The process of learning often works as a metaphor does, yoking old ideas together to make something new. In the nineteenth century, when people wanted to describe the new transportation technology that went *chug-chug-chug*, they called the engine an "iron horse" and the rail system "track way." All of these metaphors successfully conveyed a new concept by combining old concepts."

Scientists use metaphors to make sense of new scientific images and discoveries. Michael Faraday conceived of electricity as flowing liquid. Francis Crick and James Watson pictured the DNA molecules as a spiral staircase, which could split into two rungs and connect back together. Physicist Niels Bohr thought of an atom as a miniature solar system, with electrons orbiting around a central nucleus. Each metaphor provides the scientist with a model to test, analyze and develop further; proper comparisons educate and instruct. Borrowing a quality from one thing and assigning it to another puts a new perspective on our thoughts.

Do you remember the difference between similes and metaphors? Similes also compare one idea to another, but they use the expressions "like" or "as." Here's an exercise. Choose a simile from the list below and explore the relationship between the two ideas. Imagine that you had to stand in front of a group and explain the connection. Try to find five ways in which the ideas parallel each other.

Managing a project is like

Training a dog to sit and stay.
Adjusting the picture of a television set.
Wallpapering a ceiling.

Going on a vacation is like

Cleaning your basement.
Playing with modeling clay.
Enjoying a fine meal.

Finding a new job is like

Planting potatoes.
Fixing a leaky roof.
Walking through your old neighborhood.

Seeking enlightenment is like

Biting your own teeth.
Alchemy.
Opening a door which does not open.

parallel worlds

Another way of using metaphors is to put your ideas into a parallel universe. Choose a word from the list on the following page and put your idea into that world. For example, say your goal is to make significant changes at your place of work, and the word you pick is "geology." In what ways do aspects of geology, such as tectonic movement, volcanoes and different kinds of rocks, shed light on your thinking?

For fun, mathematician Thomas Hardy used to play games creating fictional cricket teams. He would, for example, create a team of women authors. For a lead batter, he would select someone who had a strong and pure voice, such as Jane Austen. Then he would fill out the rest of the team roster with authors whose writing styles would match the necessary characteristics of the team. Hardy made interesting and fruitful connections by placing his ideas into a new world.

Choose one or two worlds, preferably ones you are intimately familiar with, and put your idea into those worlds. What connections can you discover there? Remember, don't go for the logic, just search for interesting links.

parallel worlds words

Animals	Computers	**Gardening**	Mysteries
Architecture	Dance	**Geography**	Mythology
Astrology	The Desert	**Geology**	Photography
Astronomy	Economics	**Government**	Physics
The Bible	Education	**Hunting**	Plumbing
Biology	Electronics	**Insects**	Printing
Books	Entertainment	**Inventions**	Psychology
Bowling	Evolution	**Journalism**	Retail
Business	Exploration	**The Jungle**	Shakespeare
Bypass	Your Family	**Law**	Television
Camping	Farming	**Machines**	Shopping Mall
Carpentry	Fashion	**Medicine**	Space
Cars	Finance	**Military**	Sports
Children's Activities	Fine Art	**Monuments**	Weather
Comics	Fishing	**Movies**	Wine Tasting
Commercials	Flying	**Museums**	
Composers	Food	**Music**	

Step one

Write your idea on a sheet of paper.

Step two

Connect your idea to one of the phrases below in the form of a simile:

(My idea) is like (phrase).

Writing a Novel	Building a House	Exercising Your Body
Preparing a Meal	Marketing a Product	Managing a Home
Giving a Sermon	Playing a Board Game	Planning a Wedding
Camping in the Wild	Hiking in the Mountains	Raising a Child
Launching a Coup	Producing a Record	Prospecting for Gold
Fixing a Car	Hugging a Bear	Visiting the Circus
Going to a Reunion	Making Love	Climbing a Rock
Learning to Sing		

Step three

Break down the subject into parts. For example, if you chose "building a house," then consider the blueprints, foundation, contractors, location, utilities, kind of house, mortgage and so on.

Step four

Connect these features to your idea by asking questions such as: What is the house made of? Is the house large and spacious? How is the house arranged? Ask several questions to tease out the ideas.

Step five

Select three good ideas which emerge from your brainstorming. Write them down and save the list for future use.

**Use this exercise to give your metaphorical muscles
a workout.**

Personal metaphors

Fill in the blanks by completing the following metaphors:

My job is a _____ .

My body is a _____ .

My home is a _____ .

My mental life is _____ .

My relationship with my parents is a _____ .

My use of time is _____ .

Analogies

Develop an analogy for each of the following statements. Provide an explanation
for each analogy you develop.

_____ is to life as the Bible is to _____ .

A map is to _____ as a _____ is to science.

Music is to _____ as information is to _____ .

Time is to _____ as freedom is to _____ .

Relaxation is to _____ as _____ is to business.

You are your own hockey coach

Evaluate your working style by filling in the blanks below:

My weaknesses as a team would be _____.

My strengths as a team would be _____.

My half-time locker-room talk sounds like _____.

My superstars would be _____.

My bench warmers would be _____.

I would describe my coaching style as _____.

I celebrate when I win by _____.

I console and motivate when I lose by _____.

Your finances are a container

Imagine that your personal finances are embodied by a kind of container. Visualize the flow of money in and out of your financial container by answering these questions:

What kind of container do you have? _____

How does money flow in? _____

What does that money look like? (liquid, dust etc.) _____

What are the leaks in your container? _____

How big is your container? _____

How well does your container store money? _____

mixing

"THE WORLD IS TOTALLY CONNECTED.
WHATEVER EXPLANATION WE INVENT AT ANY MOMENT
IS A PARTIAL CONNECTION,
AND ITS RICHNESS DERIVES FROM THE RICHNESS
OF SUCH CONNECTIONS AS WE ARE ABLE TO MAKE."

Jacob Bronowski, Author and Naturalist

Mixing bowls, whisks and blenders are tools that combine raw ingredients. The different tools we use to mix ideas expand our creative abilities by helping us formulate new perspectives.

Tip one

Original ideas come from recognizing new connections between familiar things and transforming them into something new. Ask yourself, "How can I relate this to something I already know well?"

Tip two

Use a variety of techniques to generate new and interesting connections. Be playful. Have fun. In mixing, there's no reason not to be outrageous.

Tip three

Use metaphors, similes, analogies, comparisons and allusions to develop your ideas. What is your idea like? What can you compare it with?

cook

6

concentrate on ideas

the heat of the moment

**Concentrate on this shape while counting
from one to 100.
Try to keep your attention focused, steady
and clear for the duration of the exercise.**

fire in the mind

"JUST AS APPETITE COMES IN EATING,

SO WORK BRINGS INSPIRATION,

IF INSPIRATION IS NOT

DISCERNIBLE AT THE BEGINNING."

Igor Stravinsky, Composer

For most of us, the act of bringing a creative vision into being demands a lot of effort. We need to be able to focus our attention on the work and ignore distractions — deadlines, bills, noisy neighbors and dripping faucets.

Building and sustaining concentration is a key part of the creative process. When Thomas Alva Edison remarked, "Genius is two percent inspiration and 98 percent perspiration," he understood that discipline, perseverance and hard work form the foundation of creative endeavors. Edison knew that moments of inspiration occur during extensive periods of labor. The flashes of inspiration are great — but they happen within the context of focused work. To be inspired on a regular basis, Edison (and virtually every other creative mind) would expand, develop, refine and rework ideas.

To cook is to apply heat, and to apply creative heat is to work through the task ahead of you, seeing it through to completion. Strong and steady concentration produces results. It's the fire in the mind.

Each of us knows the experience of starting a project full of energy and commitment only to have that energy dissipate. Our interest fades and we find ourselves *trying* to concentrate rather than actually concentrating and producing. As creative individuals, we need to be able to mobilize our creative resources at will. Creative individuals seem to have the knack of summoning the muses rather than waiting around for them to appear.

Return to the opening exercise. If you didn't do it, do it now. You probably found that after a while, your attention wandered. And you probably found that every once in a while you needed to bring your attention back to the shape. That's the way our minds work. We constantly have thoughts which grab our attention and distract us. So, to keep your mind focused on the figure or any other subject, lock on to interesting aspects and ask questions. "What is this thing?" "What are the proportions?" "What does this mean?" You'll stay focused if you can maintain your interest.

But how can we turn up the creative heat and keep it hot over the course of long projects? In this chapter, we will explore a variety of ways of regulating our creative flame: adding heat and periodically allowing things to cool, finding the checks and balances to keep our intellects bubbling along at just the right temperature.

the creative flame

EXERCISE

Imagine that deep inside your mind, there is a bright creative flame burning silently, producing a radiant clear light. As you move closer, you feel its remarkable creative qualities. You sense luminescent intelligence, clarity of thought, instant responsiveness and recognition, brilliant courage and simplicity. What else might you feel as you get closer to your creative flame?

Moments of creative exhilaration often arrive suddenly and without announcement. During these times, thoughts fit together perfectly, paint flows in just the right way, music plays through our fingers. It's as if we are both a witness and a participant in the creative act.

When you tap into creative energy, everything clicks, no movement is wasted, no thought is out of place, and there is no other place you want to be. Whether you consider this state a mystical Zen-like experience or just an everyday feeling of really being in sync with your work, it certainly represents the peak creative experience.

How does the idea of a "creative flame" work? Think of the fuel which feeds the flame as the skills a person must use to meet the challenge. Think of the pot of stew to be cooked as the challenge to be met. Cooking that stew means finding the right match of fuel to the size of the pot. When you've got the right combination, your skills match the challenge and your creative juices will bubble. If there's too little fuel or the cooking pot is too large, then you are underprepared and the creative flame is too weak: you'll experience anxiety, not effortless flow. If you've got too much fuel for a tiny pot, then you are overprepared: your skills exceed the challenge and you'll feel bored, not inspired. It's what Leonardo da Vinci would experience if his greatest daily challenge was to peel potatoes.

Only when your skills match the moment perfectly, do you unleash your creative powers fully. Your creative flame burns best when you fit the challenge and the challenge fits you.

EXERCISE

Make a mind map of the factors which add to and take away from your creative energy.

146

what stokes your creative flame?

What turns your creative fire on? What keeps you really focused and intensely determined? I've asked many creative individuals these questions and received answers as varied as the people themselves. Here are a few:

Necessity

Nothing sharpens the attention better than demands.

Fun

Having a great time makes the juices flow.

Boldness

Jumping right into a situation with both feet.

Speed

Doing it as fast as you can.

Shooting from the hip

Starting without a plan and applying ideas as they come to me.

Taking a risk

A real risk without a safety net.

Feeling the crisp bite of fear

But going ahead with it anyway.

Pride

Taking pleasure in success and accomplishment.

Dread

The threat of failure lights a fire like no other.

Time pressure

The rush of a deadline.

Mental sparks

Feeling bold, standing out in the crowd and getting noticed.

Trust in last-minute inspiration

Having faith in your ability to pull the project out of the fire.

Relaxing

Loosening up the grip of life's worries.

Specialness

The knowledge that you are doing something original.

Intimacy

Having a private time, an appointment with yourself.

what douses your creative flame?

What turns your creative fire off? What causes you to lose focus or interest? The creative people I asked described many creativity extinguishers. Here are just a few:

Single thought

Relying on a single idea or plan to see your project through.

Getting really worried

Anxiety makes the creative flame burn in all the wrong places.

Not having fun

When you stop having fun, the task becomes burdensome.

Getting easily frustrated

The harder you work at being frustrated, the better you'll get at it.

Exaggerated importance

Make your challenge so important that you allow it to ruin the rest of your life.

Knowing the right answers

You're so convinced that you have all the answers that you stop entertaining alternatives.

Running it through a committee

Committees destroy individual initiative. Relying on a committee means you deny responsibility — therefore the thrill of risk is gone.

Have many meetings to discuss it

Wastes time, doubles costs.

Setting inappropriate deadlines

Make them too short and you make the task impossible; too long, and you lose interest in the project.

the flow experience

Managing creative energy involves finding balance — not the static balance you experience if you are standing stationary on one foot, but the kind of balance a surfer experiences when riding a large wave. Creative balance is dynamic and involves being sensitive and responsive to many factors.

The psychologist Mihaly Csikszentmihalyi has developed an extensive body of work describing the optimal experience — the state in which creative energy flows freely and effortlessly. His research describes that *what* people did to achieve the flow experience varied dramatically: while some people enjoyed working with their hands, others enjoyed hanging around motorcycle gangs. But *how* they enjoyed themselves was similar. When they performed activities which engaged their mind and feelings, they would enter flow. According to Csikszentmihalyi, flow occurs when the following conditions are met:

Closure

People are positively creative when they engage in tasks they have a chance of completing.

Focus

People must be able to concentrate on what they are doing.

Clear targets

People are positively creative when they engage in tasks they have a chance of completing and when they have clear goals.

Response

With these goals, they get immediate feedback within the moment-to-moment activities.

Fulfilling

While they are engaged in this activity, the focus of concentration flows into the task and away from frustrations and worries of life.

Unselfconscious

The person's attention shifts from the self, yet after the experience is over, the self is rejuvenated and feels stronger.

Expanded time

The person's experience of time is transformed; minutes expand into hours and hours can seem to pass in minutes.

The combination of these factors generates tremendously rewarding experiences: people develop a sense of control over the domain of their creative activity and of their lives. They can expend a great deal of energy just to be able to feel the creative flow. The energy that the flow experience returns makes even the most lackluster human experiences become satisfying.

Let us take a closer look at each element in the flow experience so that we can better understand how we can transform humdrum experiences into more creative expressions.

the challenging activity

Sometimes creative experiences occur haphazardly:
a passing song on a radio will trigger a flood of ideas or
inspiration. But most creative encounters occur within
goal-directed and rule-bounded activities. These activities demand skill and can range from reading (which
incorporates the skill of analysis and forming images
from words), talking politics (which involves understanding politicians' issues and positions), rock climbing (in
which the rock face becomes a chessboard of possible
approaches), to brain surgery (where the myriad of skills
require a decade or more of specialized training).

To transform an everyday activity into a flow activity,
make it more challenging. Seek competition. Set clear
and reachable goals. Develop a set of rules or constraints which give focus to your attention.

I know a public speaker who routinely challenges herself
by selecting random words and then incorporating them
into her speech. She will intentionally stumble at predetermined moments, try out longer pauses and make it a
point to look at each member of her audience. This
exercise of attention is a game she plays to keep the
activity more interesting, and it makes her a more confi-
dent speaker.

As a child, I remember deriving great satisfaction by
turning my long walk to school into an exercise of notic-
ing what was different each day. I would become familiar with each oak tree, with the shape of every house
and window and with the color of the grass. To this day
I can vividly remember the walks.

Not everyone will make the effort of inventing challenging activities. But those who do will find a place where
their level of skill meets the level of challenge, and their
creative energies are expanded. This place occurs
between the boundary of boredom and anxiety.

Tip

Adjust the level of challenge to enter flow.

immerse yourself

When your skills are engaged in dealing with the challenges of a situation, your attention becomes absorbed by the activity. Whether the flow activity is a tough game of tennis, writing an article or brainstorming an advertisement, there isn't any leftover mental energy to think about unrelated concerns. The full light of your attention is concentrated on the important and relevant stimuli.

Consequently, people become so involved in what they are doing that they become spontaneous, almost automatic in the sense that they stop being aware of themselves as distinct from the actions they are performing. The cyclist's awareness is so completely focused on riding that she is totally involved in the bike. The dancer's attention is so complete, he is only aware of music and movement. The juggler's concentration is so focused that she mentally stands back and watches her hands toss and catch the pins in syncopated rhythm.

Although the flow experience appears to be effortless, it is not. It can take a great deal of exertion to reach flow. Distractions erase concentration. In nonflow times, we continually interrupt ourselves with our internal dialogue. Our voice of judgment asks "Am I doing this correctly?" "Shouldn't I be trying to do this another way?" "I'm sure that other people are thinking that I'm not doing this very well." These continual mental interruptions clog our consciousness and bring the flow of mental energy to a grinding halt. When stoking the creative flame, we should not evaluate (unless that is the intended flow activity). Within flow there is little room to reflect.

In everyday consciousness, we tend to be tossed around by passing distractions. Worries easily flood into our minds. To enter flow, we can direct the focus of our attention on relevant stimuli and on the specific task at hand. Leave the world of worry and distraction and enter the world of involvement. Sustain concentration by attending to what's necessary and appropriate to the flow task. Find a way to do the task which leads to mental involvement.

We may learn lessons from Zen teachers. In Zen tradition, students are taught to lose themselves in the activity of the moment. A Zen student practicing archery wouldn't ask, "Am I aiming too high?" "Should I steady my breathing more?" "How can I compensate for the previous shot?" Instead the student would merge with the task. There is only doing. There is the stance, pull back and release.

Zen tradition views a person's work as a reflection of his or her state of mind. A calligrapher's brush stroke emerges from his inner state. Each stroke — whether light and wispy or bold and powerful — expresses the person's being at a particular instant. Perhaps the same could be said of our own creative work.

Tip

Keep your attention on the action.

seek immediate feedback

A hockey player will find deep involvement because the goals are clear and the feedback is immediate. In other activities where goals are less distinct, a person develops an intuitive understanding of success and failure. A pianist builds an inner gauge to sense whether a musical phrase is right or wrong. A psychiatrist creates a sense of progress and regression by attending to a patient's facial expressions, tone of voice and body language. A painter develops an eye for recognizing when a particular part of the canvas or a certain technique is good or bad.

In any open-ended creative activity, a person will create his own criteria for success as well as for progression. You may not know what the painting is going to look like in the end, but you know when you've created a painting which satisfies you. With each brush stroke, you reflect "yes, this works" or "no, this doesn't." A person needs these inner guidelines to experience flow. A person also needs this moment-to-moment sense of feedback to experience flow.

Each person finds unique goals and personal approaches within their flow activities. While some people find satisfaction in the mechanics of a car engine, others will find flow in developing ideas about medieval Russian economics. No matter what the activity, recognizing the challenges will help define the goals. The challenges and goals define a system of action and suggest the skills necessary to master it. To develop skills, you need to pay attention to the results of your actions.

Tip

Set short- and long-term goals which produce a stronger sense of flow.

an end in itself

When a task becomes important because other things are riding on it, the task usually stops being fun. When a task is satisfying and rewarding for its own sake, it often becomes a source of energy and inspiration. Hobbies produce flow because we can afford to relax with them. We enjoy these activities because — well, because we enjoy doing them. The activities we enjoy for their own sake are the ones which produce flow most strongly in us.

So turning on creative fire is a matter of finding stimulating challenges that require skill and feedback, that engage concentration fully, and that can be enjoyed for their own sake. There will be times when you want to have a lot on your plate and you want to immerse yourself in new and fulfilling creative challenges. And there will be times when you want to give yourself plenty of time to relax and unwind. We can learn to draw inspiration from the activities which naturally stimulate flow and by discovering how to produce flow in the activities we are obliged to perform.

What kinds of activities produce flow for you? Look through the following list of activities and determine what ignites your creative energy. Add any activities which you feel generates a feeling of flow for you.

Physical exertion

Cross-country skiing, running, cycling, playing football, baseball, basketball, squash, tennis, swimming, rock climbing, hiking, walking, sex, yoga, martial arts, weight training,

1. _____
2. _____
3. _____

Flow through the senses

Viewing works of art, photography, painting, listening to live or pre-recorded music, playing a musical instrument, wine tasting, cooking, giving a massage, receiving a massage.

1. _____
2. _____
3. _____

Flow of thought

Reading difficult works, exercising memory, solving crossword puzzles, writing stories, composing letters, playing your own mental games, solving philosophical problems, giving names to things, enjoying the play of words, playing with ideas in conversation. enjoying the delights of science, history and art, loving wisdom for its own sake.

1. _____
2. _____
3. _____

Flow in work

Business successes, closing a deal, making profit, gaining recognition, delivering a brilliant presentation, winning an award, satisfying a client, satisfying yourself, being more inventive, doing the job on time and under budget, being first-rate.

1. _____

2. _____

3. _____

Flow in relationships

Maintaining a romantic relationship, raising a child, deepening a friendship, spending time with family and friends, performing volunteer work, making new acquaintances, making conversations at social gatherings, hosting parties, being supportive.

1. _____

2. _____

3. _____

Flow in leisure

Exercise, reading, hunting, doodling, gardening, working around the house, enjoying friends, building model airplanes, traveling, shopping, decorating the house, working on the car, boat or lawn.

1. _____

2. _____

3. _____

Early flow

How did you enjoy flow as a child? Playing sports, riding a bike, singing, inventing control panels for spaceships, pretending to be something else, finding a secret hiding place, playing with dolls, playing dress-up, doing well in school, getting into trouble, getting out of trouble.

1. _____

2. _____

3. _____

embrace creative tension

Take a pen and a blank piece of paper and let your hand draw something completely spontaneous. Start without any preconceived image of what you are going to draw. Just let your hand do something and see what happens.

To be creative is to take a risk. Every new beginning — it could be an essay, a symphony, a computer program, a business plan — is as hard and as chancy as every other beginning. Starting a creative endeavor calls upon our courage to put ourselves on the line. For some people, the spontaneous drawing exercise is very challenging. They can't get used to the feeling of not knowing what they are going to do before they do it. And for other people, the exercise is liberating and exciting — it's a chance to let ideas flow out without inhibition.

Because we experience a chorus of moods throughout any given day, there will be times when we confront uncertainty, anxiety and the dragon of fear. Great creative individuals don't have any less fear when they stare at the blank canvas or catch a glimpse of the audience before the performance. In fact, they probably feel more. But what distinguishes them is that they consistently engage their fear, put it aside for a while, or step boldly into the heart of it, turning anxiety into energy. Action transforms fear into vitality.

The feeling of doing something without knowing where it may lead you is something a creative person learns to tolerate, appreciate and love. The seasoned creative individual can be uncertain of where he or she is going while at the same time be certain that the destination — wherever it may be — will be interesting. The less seasoned creative individual feels lost and disoriented in creative tension. With a need for quick resolve and closure, they lose sight of the need for the periodic mucking about in the dark to produce something of value.

Marvin Minsky from the M.I.T. artificial intelligence lab believes that tolerating displeasure is not only an integral part of the creative process, but central to learning. He writes, "In the early stages of acquiring any really new skill, a person must adopt at least a partly antipleasure attitude: 'Good, this is a chance to experience awkwardness and to discover new kinds of mistakes!' It is the same for doing mathematics, climbing freezing mountain peaks, or playing pipe organs with one's feet. Some parts of the mind find it horrible, while other parts enjoy forcing those first parts to work for them. We seem to have no words for processes like these, though they must be among our most important ways to grow."

Creative individuals tolerate and even thrive on this creative tension. I've seen people addicted to creative anxiety, who live in a perpetual state of turmoil, feeling continually restless, deprived, empty, and unbearably frustrated until they express their inner life in some cre-

ative way. Out of this chaos emerges something new and exhilarating.

Can we learn to enjoy feelings of tension and confusion? Certainly in moderation. To believe fully in your ability to get things done, and at the same moment to have doubts, isn't necessarily a contradiction. It is a way of walking through the creative uncertainties and managing your creative flame. Your confidence builds with every success. The more you solve problems, find ways out of dead ends and discover inspiration when you thought you had exhausted all possibilities, the more you encourage creative anxiety to stir up ideas rather than char them.

get into a creative rhythm

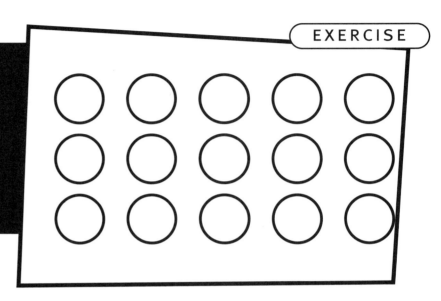

EXERCISE

Use a pen to add doodles to all circles, turning them into recognizable pictures. For example, you could draw a face, an eyeball, a button. Go ahead and complete fifteen different pictures.

Unlikely as it may seem, one of the best ways of stimulating spontaneity is through repetition. Many of us associate repetition with drudgery and conventionality — the exact opposite of creative work. However, conscious repetition can breathe fresh air on your creative flame. When you return your attention to a task over and over, you generate a rhythm which helps you tap into your genius.

The choreographer Martha Graham sometimes created new dance ideas by repeating a simple movement over and over, making minute alterations until she got something interesting. The composer Aaron Copland began musical pieces by playing one or two measures over and over, and asking "Where will this take me?" René Descartes locked himself in a dark room for days

pondering the question, "What is knowable?" and emerged with the kernel of rationalist philosophy.

Working with repetition is a dynamic cycle of expression and reflection, in which you voice an idea and then reflect on it. Then you reexpress the idea, with a difference, a variation, and reflect on it again. It's as if you take a glop of colored clay, throw it against the wall and note what happens. Then you do it again. And again, until you touch upon the germ of a new idea. This technique produces instant feedback, thereby stimulating flow.

The word "express" comes from a word meaning to press out; the word "reflect" come from a root which means to bend or turn. The entire process, which can take a fraction of a second or many months, should be dynamic — not forced and heavy. As author Michael Green writes, "There is an instant when an idea comes alive. If you freeze it too soon, it's still unformed and incomplete. Premature. But if you play around too much, you wind up with something overworked, baroque or weighty. You lose touch with the vitality of the original impulse, or cover it up so that no one else but you sees it. You have to catch the moment on the wing, so to speak."

Henry James called these germs "precious particles." When he found one, he would race to write as quickly as sentences came to mind, without any attention to spelling or structure. Similarly, when Beethoven discovered a musical idea, he would write feverishly in his notebook, sketching out variations of musical phrases, at times writing that an "idea goes here" to mark the spots he would fill in later.

When you get into a rhythm, thoughts can appear in quick, rapid-fire bursts. This is another reason for keeping a notebook. As time passes, you may or may not want to develop these germinal thoughts, but you want to keep them, just in case. These unrefined notions form the scaffolds of thought, propping up your ideas until they are firmly formulated.

Go back to the circle exercise for a moment. Did ideas come to you steadily and uniformly, say one every five seconds? Probably not. More likely, they came to you in fits and spurts. You'll get a few ideas and then run out — at which point you may have felt discouraged. But the times when you've used up your ideas are the most important. When you've run out of clichés and have no

tricks to fall back on, you are left with no choice but to pursue a genuine creative experience.

Creative dialogue occurs at all levels of creation. Each time we reencounter our subject — whether it is a painting, novel, market study or set of equations — we allow the work to mature. Repetition provides structure for successive efforts and opens the possibility of going deeper and further. As we strive for something new, reaching for the ideal, we get closer and closer, eventually finding our best solution.

A high-quality, finished product will show no sign of the tension, the wrong turns and the difficulties that went into its creation. Beethoven's symphonies flow smoothly and effortlessly. Listeners have no hint of the struggle because they did not participate in the many decisions, nor were they exposed to the countless alternatives.

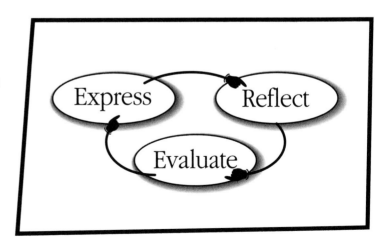

building up creative stamina

Six concentration builders:
Here are six exercises to build up mental concentration
and to strengthen your cerebral muscles.

Mental counting

Mentally recite the following sequence: Count up from two by twos until you reach 100, then down by threes until you reach one, then up by fours until you get to the largest number below 100, then down by fives, then up by sixes and so on. What is the last number in this sequence?

Two-minute attention span

Sit comfortably in front of a watch with a sweep second hand and concentrate on the motion of the second hand for two minutes. If your attention is distracted even for a moment, start again and try for two minutes.

Thought counts

Count the number of thoughts you have during a set period of time, say three minutes.

Mental monologue

In conversation, mentally repeat what someone has just said to you before you respond to them.

Thematic attention

Next time you are in a meeting, choose a particular theme and pay attention to the number of times that theme arises. Some possible themes could include excuses, distractions, winning and losing and humor.

Being there

Meditation has been called "an appointment with yourself." Take ten minutes and do nothing in particular. Just remain alert and mentally present. Why is this such a hard thing to do?

work it through puzzles

**The following puzzles can be solved by simply
spending some time working them through.
Do any of these put you into a flow state of mind?**

Trial and Error
Place 12 checkers on a six
by six grid so there are two
checkers along each row
and each column.

Mental Counting
Mentally count the number of capital letters which
contain curved lines. How many capital letters are
symmetrical about the vertical axis?

How Did They Do This?
Look at the stack of dominoes.
Can you figure out an easy way of
creating this stack?

let it cool

Take a slow deep breath.
Feel the air slowly enter your nose,
filling your lungs.
Hold it comfortably for a moment,
then allow the air out, slowly and evenly.
Count one.
Take another long deep breath and release it.
Count two.
Keep breathing in this way until you've
counted up to ten and back down again.

The nineteenth-century mathematician Henri Poincaré believed there were four stages of creative thinking. During the first stage — called preparation — you concentrate intensely on the problem at hand. If you cannot discover a solution, you put the problem aside for a while and enter the second phase — incubation. In the incubation phase, you don't do anything. You just go on with the daily business of living and assume that some part of your brain is working through the problem. If incubation is successful you reach illumination, the third phase, in which you have a sudden insight into the problem. The perception usually appears in a condensed form, a germinal thought which then needs to be developed and elaborated upon further. This fourth phase — verification — is the period in which you test the idea.

Bertrand Russell, a student of Poincaré, cultivated the incubation process through relaxing activities like walking and rowing. When he needed to write about a subject, he would think about it with the greatest intensity of which he was capable for a few hours or days. Then he would give orders to his mind that the work was to proceed underground. After some months he would return consciously to the topic and find that the work was done. Russell wrote, "Before I had discovered this technique, I used to spend the intervening months worrying because I was making no progress. I arrived at the solution none the sooner for this worry, and the intervening months were wasted, whereas now I can devote them to other pursuits."

Incubation is derived from a word which means "to lie down" or "to lie." While an idea is incubating, you relax, let go of the task at hand and do something else. Even though you may not consciously think about the subject, the machinery of your subconscious continues to work.

Everyone has experienced having a solution suddenly pop into their mind. I had solutions to computer graphic problems come to me while I was looking at bubbles in milk shakes or admiring sunsets. I didn't set out to solve the problems at those particular times. The solutions just happened to arrive during a relaxed and unfocused moment.

Sometimes a break will replenish your mental energy. Go for a walk around your neighborhood and look at the doors of the houses. Compare chimneys. Look for patterns in the trees or shrubs. Pay attention to the slight rises and dips in the sidewalks and streets.

Or, take a day trip. Drive to a nearby town you have not yet explored. When you arrive, ask around for the best place to get a chocolate sundae, or anything else that tickles your fancy. Visit the antique shops, the galleries, and wander through the back roads.

Or, take a nap. Sleep not only recharges our batteries, it allows for freer associations. After long and demanding creative sessions, remember to balance effort with rest and repose.

Or, take a bath. The nineteenth century English poet Percy Bysshe Shelley would float paper boats in his bathtub to relax his mind. Many other creative individuals soak up ideas when they soak their bodies. Creativity consultant Charles "Chic" Thompson keeps an oil based pen in his shower. When inspiration strikes, he just jots down the idea on the tiles. When it's time to clear the slate, he wipes the wall with cleanser.

Fool around. Have fun. If you've been sitting at your desk for several hours, give yourself a break by engaging your mind in some diversion. Doing something different will help renew your creative spirits.

The point of incubation is not to force ideas, but to relax and give your mind downtime. If you come up with fresh ideas, all the better. But even if you don't, you'll come back to your work refreshed if you've had some time away from the subject.

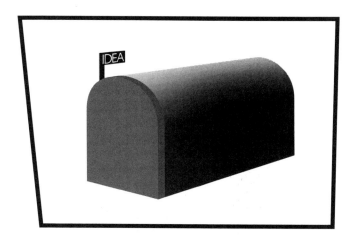

An idea dropped into the subconscious is like a letter in the mailbox.

Identify

Pose a problem and consider the consequences of solving it. Envision a world in which the challenge is solved. On a sheet of paper, write down the situation exactly as you would like it to be when your goal is realized. Describe it in the present tense in as much detail as possible. Then sit quietly, visualize the realization of your goal, put the paper away and forget about it.

Prepare

Collect information relevant to the challenge. Read, talk to others, ask questions. Immerse yourself in the problem as deeply as you can.

Incubate

Tell your brain to find the solution to the problem. Then move on to other tasks. Don't work on the problem. Eureka! The subconscious mind works at its own pace. It may take a week, a month or a year. But once the command is in your mind, it will process until the job is done. So relax and give your brain the chance to do its own thing. Return to the project periodically to check on the progress you have made.

Here is a collection of six relaxation techniques.

One

Visualize yourself in a perfect room, one that is just right for you at this moment. What would you find in this room? Who might you meet here? What conversations would you have?

Two

Visualize yourself floating on a raft on a vast calm ocean. Imagine yourself lying flat on your back looking up into a star-studded night sky. The subtle movements of the water rock you gently. A slow moving boat (which represents the return to the outside world) will arrive in ten minutes. Make the most of the time you have.

Three

Relax your muscles. Massage your shoulders, arms, legs. Roll your head around. Take a few deep breaths while you stretch your back. Visualize your body and, working from your feet upwards, feel each part relaxing. Spend ten minutes in complete repose.

Four

Repeat Technique Three, only this time, talk to yourself as if you were leading a relaxation class. Speaking the words to yourself silently in your mind gives you an anchor for your attention.

Five

Imagine that you can take a mental tour of your body. Begin by visualizing your head complete in every detail. As you bring individual features into focus, imagine that you can identify and ease away tension by gently massaging it with a mental finger. With each stroke of your finger, feel the muscles around your eyes, mouth, scalp and neck become increasingly relaxed. When your head feels refreshed, move on to the rest of your body.

Six

Visualize yourself immersed in color. Color immersion enhances the qualities and energies you'd like to possess. Although the relationship to color and emotion is purely subjective, you can use the following list described by creativity consultant Michael Michalko as a guide:

Red excites the mind and body.

Orange produces a cheerful state of mind.

Yellow encourages sensitivity.

Green provides healing and harmony.

Blue eases and relaxes the mind.

Indigo stands for creativity.

Violet produces revolutionary ideas.

How can you use color visualization to relax? Simply set aside ten or 15 minutes, sit down on a comfortable chair and breathe deeply until you feel relaxed. Choose a color and visualize it as a small ball of light in front of you. Slowly visualize the ball of color entering your body into your head and feel the color filling your skull. Watch the color massaging your body from the inside, cleansing your thoughts. Move the color through your shoulders, chest, heart, arms, legs and feet. Imagine this flow and circulate it through your body. When you feel your body immersed, suggest to yourself the desired quality. If you are visualizing the color blue, suggest to yourself how you have given yourself fully and deeply into the color. If you believe in the power of the color bath to refresh, it will become a satisfying meditation.

manage creative time

When are you at your creative peak?

Everyone has his or her own creative prime time for creativity. The 100 creative people who responded to one survey believed that they were most creative at the following times:

Showering or bathing

Working on the garden

Jogging, swimming, cycling or any kind of exercise

Driving on the highway

Mowing the lawn

Browsing through a hardware store

Listening to a talk-show program on the radio

Drifting off to sleep in the middle of the day

Commuting to and from work

Listening to a really boring lecture or meeting

Sitting on the toilet

Unfortunately, for many of us, our peak creative times don't coincide with the hours we sit at our desks, straining to produce a winning concept. Nevertheless, we all want to be able to use our creative time most effectively. Though the notion of time management may seem restrictive, in reality it is liberating: through organizing our time, we can allocate our creative resources, see that we are doing the right job and free up time for the things we really want to do.

There are several books on the market that can teach you time management systems and techniques, if you want to explore the issue in depth. Without going into a lot of detail, here are a few tips that you may find useful:

Reduce time wastage

Go back over the events of a typical day. Ask yourself: Where have I wasted my time, of other people's? What activities can I delegate or eliminate? How have other people wasted my time? Were my activities directed toward achieving my goals? If not, why not?

Set fresh goals

What can you do today that will move you closer to your long-term objectives? Make a to-do list, either at the beginning of the day or at the end of the previous one.

Rank the items according to priority. Keep this piece of paper with you throughout the day to remind you of your priorities. Remember the 80-20 rule: 80 percent of the value comes from 20 percent of the items. Do what's essential first.

Prime time

At what time of day are you at your peak? Schedule that time to work on your most important projects.

Set daily vacations

Make time for yourself. If your schedule is too full, you deprive yourself of crucial R&R time. The result: anxiety, depression and the feeling of being stuck in a rut.

Make the best of committed time

We can't eliminate the hours we spend commuting, shopping or standing in lines. But we can make better use of this time — reading, dictating to tape recorders, writing outlines and thinking up solutions to problems. We can also manage the necessary minor tasks of life — paying bills, doing housework, home repairs — by lumping them together in single blocks of time. Haphazard activity breaks up our day.

Don't always finish at the end of a work day

One of the best writing tips I ever got was from a friend who said, "When you're working really well, don't polish off the writing completely. Leave a little bit unfinished. That way, when you return to it the next day, it's easy to get back into the mood of writing. You easily complete what you did the night before and are ready to start on the next piece all warmed up."

Do what is important, not what is urgent

Have you ever had the feeling, at the end of a very busy day, that you haven't accomplished anything? Chances are you were focusing on urgent matters, rather than on issues that really count. When you are making a to-do list, focus on what is really significant, not just pressing.

One step at a time

Don't be overwhelmed by the apparent enormity of a project. The author Eric Sevareid quit his job to write a book of 250,000 words, a task that would shake even the most prolific author. His approach was to think only of the next paragraph, not the next page, and certainly not the next chapter. He said, "I never did anything but set down one paragraph after another." Six months later, the book was finished.

Serendipity time

Remember that great ideas can strike when our minds are relaxed and unfocused. When does inspiration strike you?

Stay playful

When you joke around, you free your mind to consider off-the-wall possibilities — after all, you're just kidding. Having fun helps you to silence the inner judge which condemns ideas as absurd. In creative work, being playful makes good sense.

Maintain a variety of projects

One of the keys to building resilience is to organize your work so that you always have a variety of things to turn to. Shifting focus will help prevent you from becoming bored, and the work you do in one area may be applicable somewhere else too.

Spend time at a hobby

What do you enjoy doing for its own sake? Hobbies stimulate the mind; take time to pursue your interests and you'll return to your work refreshed.

Spend time with people

Immerse yourself in a supportive environment. Find people who are not just sympathetic to your endeavor, but who understand your purpose and who can offer real advice. Look for people who will challenge you constructively. Don't be afraid to try out new ideas before they are fully baked. Your idea doesn't have to sound poetic or be in its final form. Ask honest questions and be open to the answers.

Persevere

Keeping ideas coming may just be a matter of cranking out material. Bach wrote a cantata every week, even when he was tired or sick. Some of the pieces are better than others, and some borrow heavily from his earlier works. But every week he added something new. Bach understood that the creative muscles need to be exercised regularly.

Pretend that you are feeling creative

When all else fails, trick yourself into getting into the creative mood. Position yourself as you would if you really were concentrating.

managing creativity in the workplace

Businesses spend millions of dollars each year training employees to improve their professional skills. They spend very little on developing creativity — even though more than half of the top executives interviewed in a 1992 study believed that creativity in business was more important than intelligence.

Nevertheless, whether or not you send employees on creativity courses, there are steps you can take to encourage creative thinking at your workplace. You can try to reduce the creativity killers: meetings, paperwork, constant interruptions. You can demonstrate your support of individual self-expression — holding, for example, a contest for "best-dressed workspace." But above all, you can show employees that you feel their ideas are important. When people feel valued and see their ideas adopted, they feel that they are making a real contribution — and are encouraged to participate more.

Meanwhile, *you* may be a creativity killer and not even know it. Take a look at the list on the next page. Do any of these phrases look familiar? Avoid using them: they're all surefire ways of nipping creative ideas in the bud.

A recent study in a large corporation was implemented to make people feel that they are creative. The study determined that the single factor which separated creatively productive people is that they saw themselves as creative. When a person sees themselves as creative, they are willing to put themselves into the creative frame of mind. The management company then realized they simply needed to encourage people to see themselves as creative.

A 1992 study interviewed 100 top business executives of Fortune 500 Companies and Inc. Magazine's 50 fastest growing companies to illustrate the attitudes about creativity today. When asked which was more important in business — intelligence or creativity — 59 percent voted for creativity, compared to 28 percent who believed intelligence.

thirty phrases that kill creativity

"It's too much work."
    "It hasn't been done before."

"Don't rock the boat."
    "Get your head out of the clouds into reality."

"Yeah. We've tried that before."
    "You have a point, but..."

"It costs too much."
    "That isn't your problem."

"We don't have the time."
    "Good idea, but it's impractical."

"They won't buy it."
    "That doesn't concern you."

"It'll never get past the union."
    "You will never get it off the ground."

"We haven't budgeted for it."
    "Stay in your place."

"You are ahead of your time."
    "It's too radical."

"It won't pay for itself."
    "You can't teach an old dog new tricks."

"It won't work."
    "Let's put that idea on the back burner now."

"We have always done it this way."
    "It would take too much effort."

"Management will have problems with it."
    "Don't be a dreamer."

"Oh no. Not that idea again."
    "We'll become laughing-stocks!"

"Where did you dig that one up?"
    "We did fine without it before."

cooking

"IN CREATIVE WORK, A SINGLE PRODUCT IS JUST A
TEMPORARY RESTING PLACE IN THE CONTINUOUS
AND DEMANDING PROCESS.
THE CONTRADICTORY PULLS OF JOY AND DISCOUR-
AGEMENT, OF SUDDEN BURSTS OF INSIGHT AND
TIRING EFFORTS OF EXECUTION, OF PROCESS AND
PRODUCT, ARE THE NECESSARY TENSIONS THAT
FUEL CREATIVE THOUGHT."

Vera John-Steiner, Psychologist

Large, complex creative projects require commitment.
You must be prepared to make the work part of your
life and to put in the effort required to see it through
to fruition. Above all, you must be ready to dedicate
your two most important resources to the task: time
and energy.

Tip one

Work through your ideas. Express and reflect upon
them. This is not always an easy process. Along the way
there will be wrong turns, and at times you may need to
throw away some of your work. But also remember the
heat of creation makes the product better; the sustained
effort forces you to reach further and to dig deeper.

Tip two

Sustain concentration by focusing on your purpose.
Visualize your objective, keep it in front of you, and use
it as a guide to manage your time and energy.

Tip three

Give yourself time to incubate the idea. Let it go for a
while and spend some time on other things. Trust your
subconscious to keep up the work. And be ready to
grasp your idea when it comes.

spice

7

season ideas

what if...?

What if people had four arms?
How might things change?

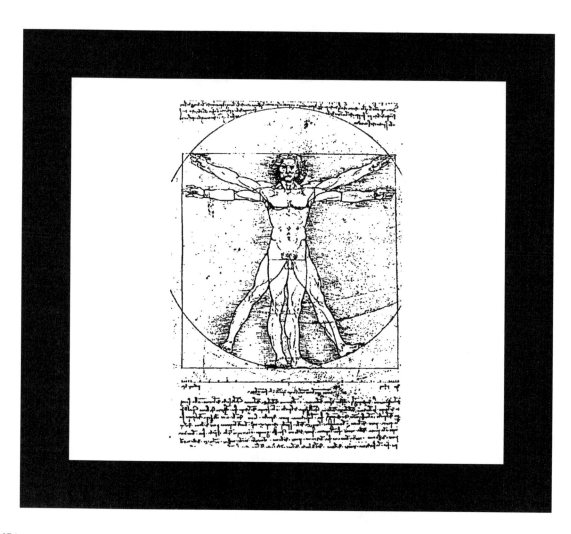

pepper, ginger, salt, nutmeg

"WE CAN REVIVE THE SPIRIT OF INVENTIVENESS
BY ALLOWING OURSELVES THE FREEDOM
TO CONSIDER THE UNCONVENTIONAL AND
PROBE THE POSSIBILITIES OF THE IMPOSSIBLE."

John Barell, Author

Although life calls upon us to be sensible, practical, realistic, and at times cynical, creativity thrives when we zealously look for the unusual and offbeat. Many creative individuals keep a tab on bizarre subjects for their personal edification. Creativity consultant Roger von Oech collects vintage television commercials. In the original score of Mozart's Horn Concerto #4 (K. 495), the inks divide into four colors, playfully arranged through the music. Although Mozart did this for visual effect only, he is not the only creative individual who enjoyed fooling around. Creative individuals easily switch into play; they like to listen to music, look at art, read, dance, play with children, travel, visit friends and shoot baskets.

These outside activities contribute material which allows you to sidestep clichés and to freshen up ideas. Splashing in some "extra ingredient" adds zest, flavor and life to our ideas, and brings out hidden flavors. Spices are the extra ingredients which transform a good dish into a great entrée.

As in cooking, creative spicing is highly personal. The chef tastes and thinks, "Hmm. It needs a certain something..." and then opens the spice cabinet. In creative thinking the spices are the interesting approaches, stories, memories and ideas which awaken the inner palate of the imagination, challenge and tease, tickle and season and whet the appetite.

Creative individuals like to play within their work, as well. An artist may toss paint on the fabric and pour on household chemicals to see what happens. The computer programmer may add a little routine that counts useless information. The writer toys with words and characters. The architect plays with kids' blocks.

Fooling around can make you giggle, provide a new way of looking at things and open the door to something different. Having fun keeps your thinking light and limber. And, as a result, many creative ideas and solutions emerge from playful speculation. Exploring a train of unlikely ideas gets you into that "anything goes" frame of mind where you are quick to see new possibilities.

Recently, a manufacturer of dinner plates had a problem. The plates were packed in boxes with old newspapers. Every packer would eventually slow down to read the papers and look at the pictures. Most employees would drop to about 30 percent efficiency. The managers tried several incentives to keep the workers focused, but after several hours or days, everyone would pick up reading the paper.

In a brainstorming session, the managers came up with several solutions: change the language of the newspaper — but where would they get these papers, in quantity? Use other materials — but the newspapers were free and they didn't have the budget. Award incentives for the number of plates wrapped — that didn't work. Then one manager suggested, "What if we poked out the eyes of the packers?" Although the suggestion sounded ridiculous, it eventually led to the idea of hiring blind people. The blind packers easily did the job without being distracted. The company also provided a valuable service to the community.

What did you come up with in the "What if...?" exercise? If people had four arms, glove sales would double. Secretaries could learn to type on two typewriters at once. Mechanics would drop fewer screws, and construction workers could saw and hammer at the same time. Tools would change, as would fashions, car designs and the rules for basketball and poker. Because of this extra capacity, the human brain might have evolved differently. In addition to a left and right brain, we might have developed extra front and back brains.

Edward de Bono writes, "If the purpose of chance in generating new ideas is to provide one with something to look at which one would not have looked for, then there may be methods of encouraging this process. Play is probably the ideal method. It must, however, be purposeless play without design and direction. Just as a carefully designed experiment is an attempt to jerry nature along the path of logical investigation, so play is an attempt to encourage the chance appearance of phenomena which would not be sought out. Playing around is an experiment with chance."

"What if?" questions can begin with a moment of wonder or a passing thought. They open our imagination to entirely new possibilities and encourage the mind to wander playfully, unfettered by the need to come up with something productive.

Creativity thrives in an environment of fun, anecdote, off-the-wall connections, double meanings, trivia, puns — anything which makes you look at life in a slightly different way. Have fun with games, puzzles, quizzes and stories. And who knows, you might be able to incorporate some of these fun things in your work.

For starters, ponder the following "What if?" questions. Use them as springboards to dream of things that never were and say, "Why not?" Get your mind on a roll and come up with your own set of "What if?" questions.

What if the day suddenly became 26 hours long?

How would this affect our work day? Would we spend more time cramming in activities during the day or would we spend more time engaged in leisure? How would watch and clock designs change to accommodate the extra hours? Would the hours be added in at night or in the middle of the day? Would people be happier because they got more sleep at night and feel more rested? Would life spans be longer (because there was more rest) or shorter (because people would live fewer days since there were more hours each day)?

What if you won a million dollars?

Would you strive to make long-term changes or have a lot of fun for a short while? What single possession have you always wanted to acquire? What dreams would you try to fulfill?

What if the bubonic virus had been deadlier?

Science fiction author Robert Silverburg wrote an alternate history in which 60 percent of Europe's population died of the plague in the fourteenth century, rather than the actual 30 percent. In this alternate world, Europe did not have the manpower to repel the invading Turks. As a result, there was no Renaissance, all of Europe was under Islam and the New World was not plundered: the Aztec and Mayan civilizations dominated the land.

What if people had no fear?

If everyone suddenly lost their fears — fear of failure, fear of change, fear of loss — would the Earth be a better or worse place to live? Would there be social unrest as employees told their bosses what they really thought? Would families become more intimate because they could communicate better? Would daredevils be in demand or out of jobs?

What if you could have any single wish come true?

If a genie appeared and granted you any single wish, what would you want to have happen? Would you want to change yourself in any way? Physically? Mentally? Emotionally? Spiritually? Would you want boundless knowledge or power? Would you change the world? Restore the Earth's environment? Would you visit the rest of the galaxy?

What if you couldn't ask "what if" questions?

If you couldn't envision things which don't exist, could you still be creative? Maybe accident would be the main driving force in creative thought, and the development of science and art would be a process of evolution; a successful endeavor would be retained because it worked. Would not being able to get "what if" questions be like some people's inability to get metaphors, allusions or to see beauty in flowers or in art?

the languages of thought

"THE WORDS OF THE LANGUAGE,
AS THEY ARE WRITTEN OR SPOKEN,
DO NOT SEEM TO PLAY ANY ROLE
IN MY MECHANISMS OF THOUGHT.
THE PHYSICAL ENTITIES WHICH SEEM TO SERVE
AS ELEMENTS IN THOUGHT ARE CERTAIN SIGNS
AND MORE OR LESS CLEAR IMAGES WHICH
CAN BE VOLUNTARILY REPRODUCED OR COMBINED."

Albert Einstein, Physicist

What distinguishes one creative process from another — and the scientist from the artist — are the inner languages of people's thoughts. Human thought is a very complex, interwoven fabric of abstract and representational images, partly formed feelings and streams of words. It is a weave of inner dialogues, reveries, daydreams, preoccupations, crystallized concepts, half-formed opinions, fleeting thoughts and long-term values. Creative individuals know how to manipulate the symbols of their chosen languages.

Each language of thought represents a different way of knowing and of thinking. Each of us is familiar with these languages in varying degrees. They are rooted in our perceptions: in our senses of touch, sight and hearing; in movement and balance; and in imagination:

Words

For many of us, words — spoken, written and internally formulated — represent the most familiar of inner languages. Words bridge many parts of experience, connecting past and future, thought and feeling, comment and action.

Images

Mental images are inner facsimiles of objects of sense. Visual thinking is the manipulation of these images as diagrams, pictures, models, storyboards, moving pictures.

Music

Music is said to be the universal language, the language of emotion which crosses all borders, all times, all divisions and partitions of human culture.

Movement

Kinesthetics plays a role in choreography, in facial expressions, in a basketball player's fake or a skateboard move. In dance, emotional statements are made through physical movements.

Abstract thought

Abstract thought attempts to divorce itself from the world of perceptions. Mathematics is the prime example; its language is concerned with relationships, calculation and logical reasoning.

These categories are not absolute divisions, but convenient descriptions. A scientist may use verbal, visual and abstract reasoning to solve a problem. A choreographer may use kinesthetic images to score a dance, and visual images to conceive how the audience will perceive the dance. An author will flip between a core theme or image and the flow of words.

British scientist Grey Walter claims that 15 percent of people think primarily with words, 15 percent use images, and the remaining 70 percent rely on a combination of words and images. Author Morton Hunt puts it this way: "We do not always think in words, but we do little thinking without them."

We can add the technique of translating from one mental language to another to our creative thinking tool kit. When we want to spice up our ideas, we can switch to another mode of thinking and express our ideas through a new medium. How might we go about doing this?

from one pot to another

DOES HE PAINT?

HE FAIN WOULD WRITE A POEM,

DOES HE WRITE?

HE FAIN WOULD PAINT A PICTURE.

Robert Browning, Poet

Don Campbell, author of *Introduction to the Musical Brain,* once had to teach the letters of the alphabet to a group of learning disabled students. Other instructors had dismissed the task as impossible, since the students could not write out the letters. But Campbell took a different approach. He had the students sketch out the letters with their bodies. They walked around the letters, drew them with their elbows and danced them one after another. By the end of a single class, all the students could recite the entire alphabet.

Sometimes, using only one language of thought can get a person stuck. At the turn of the century, when physicists were exploring the nature of the atom, many were inadvertently bound by the meaning of the word itself. The word "atom," derived from the Greek, means "indivisible." The physicists had to break free of this concept to show that the atom was in fact composed of constituent parts.

Words tend to fix ideas in place. They give us solid handles of thought. The Gestalt psychologist, Rudolf

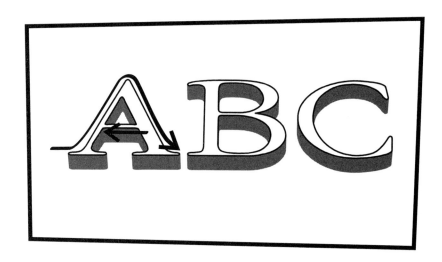

Arnheim, suggests that verbal language is essentially "stabilizing and conservative." Words are sequential; they string out experience into cause and effect, into a series of events, into a pattern bound by the flow of time. The old Latin expression, "Nomen est Numen" — to name is to know — expresses the idea that words fix concepts. In a way, when an idea has a name, we have cast it in plaster: it becomes fixed, familiar, with specific properties.

Imagery, on the other hand, tends to be more flexible than words. Changing our point of view is as easy as closing one eye, looking and then closing the other eye and looking again. Visual images often appear rapidly, and encourage a sense of playfulness and discovery. A single image can yield a wealth of meanings. While the image of a branching tree meant one thing to Darwin, it can represent almost anything, from a genealogical chart, to a river pattern, to a neural network, to the way water flows down your driveway after you wash your car.

Each language has its own syntax and structure. English, for example, follows a subject/verb/object pattern. Mathematics derives its power to make subtle proofs from the precise rules of logic. While imagery is subjective and inferential, there are principles governing good composition and meaningful juxtaposition of visual elements.

Leonard Bernstein compared musical structure and meaning to spoken language: the musical motifs correspond to nouns; chords are the modifiers; and rhythms act like verbs. Composer Cedric Thorpe Davie also understands the relationship between music and language: "The musical phrases, the smallest intelligible musical units, offer as much satisfaction as a line of poetry. The intellect and feelings need that two or more phrases be put together to balance one another and to add to one another's meaning: as in literature, where logically connected clauses are built up into intelligible sentences, so in music the first step towards the making of continuous sense consists in putting together two or more phrases to make a musical sentence."

Expressing your idea in another language of thought is another way of getting a new perspective on your work. In this way, a novelist can look for musical harmony, progression, surprise, contrast and balance in a thriller, and the musician can develop a conversation — statement and response — in a melody. The artist searches for logic in the painting, and the mathematician is sensitive to the beauty and elegance of a logical proof. Try switching languages yourself using the exercises on the following pages:

words

Sixty-second stories

Improvize for a minute about how you might deal with the following situations. Go ahead and actually describe what you would do.

- You've been set up on a blind date by a friend. You've seen a picture of this person and know that he (or she) is very attractive. It's a few minutes before your date arrives and you walk into the bathroom to discover you've got a huge pimple on your nose.

- You're a fashion model in the dressing room making a quick change and are due on the runway in a few moments. As you slip on the outfit, you rip off the left sleeve.

- You've met an attractive person of the opposite sex at a party and told them that you are a famous artist. You get a call from this person who is at the ground floor of your studio apartment wanting to pay a social visit. There is not a single painting in your apartment.

- Your spouse finally unveils the surprise weekend event that he/she has been planning for a month — bungee jumping.

- You're a member of the space shuttle crew and just as you enter orbit, you realize that you've forgotten something very important.

Sixty-second speeches

These improvizations are great fun at the family dinner table. Choose a theme and forcefully explain and defend it in one minute.

- Diamonds are wonderful, but it's better to wear unpolished rocks.

- War is inevitable. There is absolutely nothing that can be done to prevent armed conflict when things get tense.

- It's far more important to get an education in music and art than it is to concentrate on reading and writing.

- It's fine for little kids to play with matches.

- Chicken Little was absolutely correct: the sky is falling.

- I am really from the future, 1,000 years from now.

- There's no question that television is the best invention ever.

- People shouldn't have sex until they are 25 years old.

- Accountants are the most creative people in the world.

- Red is the worst color in the rainbow.

- Everyone in the world should, by law, speak English.

Mysterious questions

Pose these questions around the dinner table as a starting point for verbal exploration:

- What are the three most important things the leader of a country does?

- What does it really mean to be beautiful?

- If you could travel back into history and live there for a period of one year, what three items would you take with you? Why?

- What are two impossible things — events that simply could not happen?

- How can you tell if someone is not telling the truth? What are the signs?

- Do dreams really mean anything? Where do they come from?

- Who has more fun — men or women? Why?

New product names

Marketing people are continually in need of names which catch people's attention. Come up with clever, marketable names for the following new products:

- An ultrathin computer monitor

- An aerosol spray which perfumes your clothes.

- A video and book guide which teaches teenagers the value of keeping off drugs.

- An inflatable snow sled.

- Umbrella hats which are designed to reduce exposure to ultraviolet radiation.

- Jewelry which is designed to carry condoms — discretely.

- Modern-day tarot cards.

- A paint that continually changes color over a period of several hours.

New slogans

Often as important as a name is a product's slogan. Come up with a winner slogan for the following products or companies:

- A pen that has double the ink capacity of normal pens.

- A word processor program that specializes in correcting spelling mistakes as you type.

- A light bulb that lasts six times longer than other light bulbs, but is twice as expensive.

- A restaurant that lets customers cook their own dinner at a large grill. The grill is in the dining area and encourages the customers to mingle as they grill.

- A shopping mall which combines the features of arcades, science centers and museums in an attempt to develop a niche market called educational shopping. Shoppers can look at gemstones, art and buy sneakers all on the same floor.

- A telephone with a computerized ringer which can play up to twenty digitally sampled sounds including a violin, a fire truck siren, a cat's meow and a shotgun blast.

ABCD Thinking

Can you find an everyday word which can be formed from four consecutive letters in the alphabet?

Thingamabobs

Did you know that the shaft on top of an umbrella is called a ferrule, and that the two buttons a telephone receiver rests on are called plungers? The following list of dohickies, gizmos and whatchamacallits are genuine words and are names of common objects. While you read them, assign them to particular objects.

Aglet

Bail

Bobeche

Bollard

Finial

Forel

Neb

Pintle

Tang

Zarf

Intrinsic names

In an experiment conducted by psychologist J. P. Guildford, when people have the choice of assigning the names "wanesh" and "tuckatee" to the following two shapes, most name the angular shape "tuckatee."

Look around the room now and choose any three objects and give them names which feel right.

Visualization warm-up

Select a nearby object — a book, say, or a lamp — and spend several minutes considering it from different points of view. Can you picture what it would look like upside down, from a few millimeters away, from the rear? What might you see if you could travel through it? Allow yourself to discover new possibilities.

Mental cubism

Mentally fold these six squares into a cube. Can you picture it clearly?

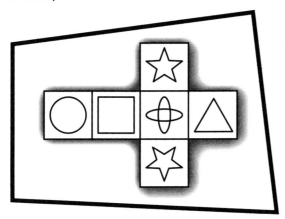

Mental dice

Mentally hold each die in front of you. Can you turn them around, see them from different perspectives?

Envision

Imagine the following ideas:

- Visualize the way from your house to work.

- Visualize ten faces.

- Visualize five hotel rooms you've been in.

- Visualize five animals that begin with the letter "B."

- Visualize five lamps.

- Visualize five car interiors.

- Visualize five kinds of clouds.

Close Packing

What is the greatest number of identical bowling balls you can pack around a central bowling ball so that each ball touches the central ball?

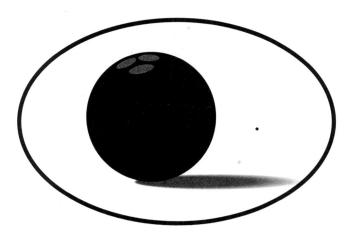

Envision

- The way from your house to work

- A picture of yourself successful

- A picture of yourself happy, relaxed and fulfilled

- A picture in your mind of you ten years from now

- A picture of yourself 20 pounds heavier (thinner) than you are

- A picture of yourself doing something that you've dreamed of doing

- A picture of yourself with enough money in the bank

- A picture of starting an ideal job

Virtual walk-through

Visualize this room and imagine walking through it.

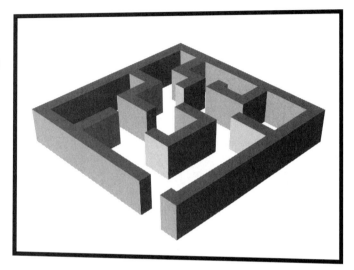

The big walk

Imagine that the following shape is the size of a football field. Can you picture walking around its periphery?

Practical visualization

The Australian psychologist Alan Richardson conducted a remarkable experiment connecting visualization and sports performance. Three groups of students, none of whom had any experience with visualization, were chosen at random to play basketball. The first group practiced free throws for twenty days. The second group practiced only on the first and twentieth days. The third group also practiced on the first and twentieth days, but also spent twenty minutes per day visualizing that they were making baskets.

The visualizers were told to focus on the texture of the experience. The students imagined feeling the ball in their hands, walking up to the line, sighting the basket, judging the throw, feeling the motion of the throw and hearing the sound of the ball. If the ball made a clean pass through the net, they heard that sound. If the ball bounced off the rim to the floor, they heard the bounce. When they missed a shot, they adjusted their aim until they could consistently make the shot.

The first group, who practiced with real basketballs, improved by 24 percent. The second group, who did next to no practicing, did not improve at all. And the third group, the visualizers, improved by 23 percent. For hardly touching a real basketball, that's pretty impressive.

How do creative minds use visualization? Napoleon imagined himself on the battlefield before stepping into battle. Conrad Hilton picturered himself owning a hotel before he actually bought one. Dr. Charles Mayo mentally rehearsed performing an operation before he suited up. The mental rehearsal readies the mind and frees the imagination to roam where it wants to, and to confront the future. When you ask what you want as the final result, try formulating the answer as a mental picture. Your answer could be a picture of a novel sitting on the best-seller stand. It could be an image of a completed painting or an image of four close friends enjoying a lunch on your newly renovated deck. It might be a picture of your students getting a concept and lighting up. When you know what you want as the end result, you give yourself direction. Hold that picture in your mind and you will draw yourself toward it. Make your image clear, vivid and steady and your target becomes even more distinct. Remember that every great work began as an image in someone's imagination.

kinesthetic images

Moving visualizations

Visualize the sensations you would experience in the following situations and activities:

- A teenager going to a new school for the first time
- Jumping out of an airplane with a parachute
- A student who has just received an A+ instead of the expected D
- Someone who has just been fired
- A child chasing a balloon
- Riding an Olympic bobsled
- A rookie policeman after making the rounds
- Snorkeling in a barrier reef
- Piloting an F-16 jet fighter

Abstract images

Answer the following questions by tapping into your abstract imagination:

- Which is bigger, red or brown?
- Which is more massive, stretch or yawn?
- Which occupies more space, a laugh or a sneeze?
- Which is funnier, Q or Z?
- Which is slower, might or courage?
- Which takes more energy, an acorn or light?
- Which is more accommodating, the sky or a century?
- Which creates more fear, flat or curved?
- Which has more energy, ‹ or › ?

**Consider the world 25 years from today.
In the following list of questions, incorporate each kind
of thinking — visual, verbal, kinesthetic and abstract
— into the formulation of your ideas.**

What will a personal computer look like?

How will have cars changed?

What will conservative dressers be wearing?

What will a TV look like? What programs will be shown?

How will society deal with violent crime?

What will society consider the ideal body type for a man, woman and child?

Which job skills will be most in demand? How will they be taught?

How will health care have changed?

What sort of self-help programs will be popular?

How will the world map have changed?

What will be on the news tonight?

**Answer these questions with ingenuity and imagination and you
will be considered to be a visionary.**

Practice translating an idea into different languages.

Step one

Identify an objective and formulate a mission statement. Write down a sentence which describes your goal.

Step two

Translate your statement into an image. Don't worry about realism; just draw something which links you to your goal. For example, if your aim is to get a new car, draw a picture of the ignition key, or your view of the dashboard, or of a scene from your first country drive in the new car. Make your picture an image of the future. Write down your intended completion date above or below the drawing.

Step three

Make a model. Using any solid medium — clay, toothpicks, lego blocks, mashed potatoes — make a three-dimensional representation of your objective.

Step four

Draft a flowchart. At one end of a piece of paper, draw a rectangle to show where you are. At the other end, draw one that shows where you want to be. Then fill in the space between with shapes that represent intermediate steps.

Step five

Formulate an equation. Arrange the various elements affecting your goal into a balanced equation. On one side place the goal, and on the other side arrange the factors which will add up to your objective.

Step six

Dance your idea. What type of gesture can you make to express your goal. Consider walking, climbing, jumping up and down, punching something, lying down and relaxing, doing some exotic dance. How does your body understand your objective?

intuition

EXERCISE

Who is going to call you on the telephone?

Have you ever had the intense feeling that you knew something without knowing why you knew it? For example, have you ever avoided a business deal — for no explicit reason — only to hear later that it turned out badly for someone else? Have you ever looked at a ringing phone and known who was at the other end?

Unlike logical, sequential, analytic thinking, intuition uses insight, imagination and guesswork to solve problems. Intuition is vital when you need to make choices based on incomplete information. Think back to some decisions you made in the past. Consider the options that were open to you at the time. How did you reach your decision? Did facts which come to light afterwards bear you out?

How in tune are you with your intuition? Try asking yourself the following questions:

Telephone calls

The next time the telephone rings, before you answer it, ask yourself who the call is from. After you answer, try to guess the nature of the call before the person tells you.

Work

How many sales will you close today? What will your colleagues at the office be wearing? When you first visit people with whom you've only talked on the phone, try to imagine what they and their offices will look like.

Meetings

What mood will be the participants be in? How will different individuals respond to information? Who will be supportive? Who will be negative? What questions will they ask?

Recognizing that you have intuitive powers is one thing; learning to rely on them in decision making is something else again. It may help you to know that many important people — among them George Washington and the founder of Eastman Kodak, George Eastman — often trusted their intuition during their careers. According to the findings conducted by the International Institute for Management in Lausanne, Switzerland, successful managers claim they often use intuition in their major business decisions.

Just as there are languages of thought, there are languages of intuition. Each person has highly personalized ways to tap into his or her intuition. For some people, intuitive connections are kinesthetic; they experience tactile sensations, a tension in the shoulders, a sense of heat or coldness, a feeling of dizziness. For other people, the intuition talks to them through voices in their head. They might hear "something inside me says not to believe that person." For visual people, the intuition appears through unexpected images.

Intuition can be clear or the messages can be cluttered, and we just need to spend some time unraveling what our intuition tells us — and to trust in that intuition. In this way we communicate with our muses — those unintentional images of power and sensitivity. Professor George Turne from the University of California, Berkeley, writes that the central features of intuition and problem solving are:

- The ability to know how to attack a problem without knowing how you know
- The ability to relate a problem in one field to seemingly different problems in unrelated fields
- The ability to see links, connections and relationships between ideas and objects
- The ability to recognize the cause of a problem
- The ability to see in advance a general solution to the problem
- The ability to recognize solutions because they feel right
- The ability to focus on what may be rather than what is

Exercises to stimulate intuition

A terrific guessing game, one which engages imagination, logic and intuition, is called Essences. Two or more players agree on a subject — say, famous people. One person thinks of a person, then the others try to identify that character by guessing his or her "essence." The play of the game might progress as follows:

Okay, I am thinking about a male historical character.
(The subject is Albert Einstein.)

Q: **What musical instrument is this person?**

A: A violin.

Q: **What color is this person?**

A: Light grey, with splashes of purple.

Q: **What clothing is this person?**

A: A rumpled sweater.

Q: **What body of water is this person?**

A: A still lake but with great undercurrents beneath.

Q: **What kind of tree is this person...?**

Answers are not right or wrong: they express your impression of that person.
Think about the questions you might ask if you were dealing with the following categories:

What colour?	What flavor of ice cream?	What period of history?
What body of water?	What animal?	What kind of music?
What article of clothing?	What facial expression?	What kind of food?
What kind of car?	What kind of city?	What kind of television show?
What kind of weather?	What typeface?	What kind of plant?
What period of architecture?	What beverage?	What style of literature?
What style of art?	What sport?	What part of a house?
What kind of movie?	What time of the day?	What part of the body?

encourage luck

"NAME THE GREATEST
OF ALL INVENTORS:
ACCIDENT."

Mark Twain, American Novelist

Creative people seem to have all the luck. Sir Alexander Fleming accidentally dropped some bread mold into a culture of bacteria, contaminating the mixture. Cursing his luck, he looked at the petri dish under a microscope anyway, and saw within the sea of bacteria islands of clear regions. Fleming discovered that the mold prevented bacterial growth. The mold was penicillin. A stroke of luck, but Fleming was ready for it.

Creative individuals seem to have a knack of being in the right place at the right time. A new piece of information comes across the desk. The newspaper article pro-vides the missing clue. An associate whom you haven't seen in ten years attends the conference and has the rights to distribute the product you need. Things just work out.

We think this kind of good fortune as a lucky flash of lightning — uncontrollable and impossible to predict. But as author Denise Shekerjian writes, "A more accurate assessment would be if a person went to the hardware store, bought the best lightning rod he could find, climbed to the highest point on his roof, bolted the contraption in place, and then waited patiently next to it for a storm."

Luck comes to those who are searching for something. Never underestimate its value. Consider how many people combined luck with an attentive eye to develop their ideas:

Vulcanized rubber

For several years, Charles Goodyear searched for an industrial use for rubber. The problem was that rubber was too soft when hot and too brittle when cold. One day, he accidentally spilled some rubber on the stove; it baked into a dark, hard substance. The new rubber was consistently strong and pliable — at many temperatures. Goodyear discovered the process of vulcanization.

Saccharin

In the year 1879, chemist Constantin Fahlberg scratched his lip in the lab, without washing his hands. He was overwhelmed by a remarkably sweet taste. Several years later, the substance became a substitute for sugar.

X rays

At the turn of the century, physicist W. C. Roentgen conducted a series of experiments using cathode ray tubes. Nearby, he had left a sheet of paper covered with a chemical called barium platinocyanide for another experiment. To Roentgen's surprise, whenever he turned on the cathode ray tube, the paper glowed. He went on to discover the X ray.

Electromagnetism

While demonstrating magnetism to a science class in 1819, Hans Christian Oersted passed a wire between the poles of a horseshoe magnet. He noticed that whenever he moved the wire, it gave off a bit of electrical currents. Oersted went on to demonstrate the connection between electrical current and magnetism, and eventually paved the way for the development of the electric motor and generator.

Nitrocellulose

C. F. Schonbein, an inventor, was trying to make a stronger, yet easier to handle gun powder. Working in his kitchen, he accidentally spilled some nitric acid and wiped it up with his wife's apron. A few minutes after he hung the apron over the stove to dry, it burst into flames (and nearly burned down his house). The incident eventually led him to the discovery of nitrocellulose, a substitute for gun powder.

These stories show how important it is to always be on the look-out for, and open to, new ideas. But there are thousands of accidents every week. How do we know which to pursue? We don't always. But if we trust in our intuition and listen for the messages it tries to convey to us, we will at least be open to the possibilities. Make room for some accidents to happen, attend to them closely, pick out the useful ideas, and you'll become a luckier person.

encourage luck

The following collection of diversions, curiosities and musings can spice up your thinking. Who knows where you might find an idea which brings out the flavor of a problem you are working on.

Character expressions

People who communicate with computers on line have developed a series of expressions for communicating emotions. The expression :) represents a happy face. (Just imagine the expression turned 90 degrees clockwise.) The expression :(is a sad face. The expression :/ is a frown. ;) is a wink. . -) has one eye. :-t is angry. :-? is smoking a pipe. :-' has a cold. :-D talks too much. :-O is shocked. :-% has a beard. (-: is left handed. {(:-) is wearing a toupee. }(:-) is wearing a toupee in the wind. [:-) is wearing a walkman. :~) needs a nosejob. :-)8 is well dressed. %-^ is Picasso.

Neat science experiments

Every kid likes science experiments, the kind where you start with a problem and work to a solution.

You can pick up an ice cube with an ordinary cotton string by wetting the string, resting it on the ice and sprinkling it with salt. The salt lowers the freezing point on the ice causing the less salty water in the string to freeze and become attached to the cube.

It's possible to make a flame appear to jump magically. Light a candle and let it burn for a few minutes. Blow out the candle and hold a lit match in the rising smoke two inches above the wick. The flame will travel down the smoke and light the candle. The smoke is actually made of vaporized wax that is almost at its kindling point. In a coal mine, a flame may travel more than a kilometer in a few seconds along a mixture of vapor.

Burn a lump of sugar by sprinkling cigarette ash on it first. Normally, the sugar cube will not easily burn. The ash prevents the sugar from cooling, and acts like a catalyst, helping the chemical reaction without changing itself.

Rules of thumb

In a wonderful book, *Rules of Thumb*, author Tom Parker has compiled a list of guesses, formulas and distilled wisdom. Here are a few:

A half-hour network news broadcast reduced to type will fill about half the front page of a newspaper.
ROGER CARPENTER, NEWSBUFF

When setting up an aquarium, provide at least one gallon of water for each inch of fish.
JEFF FURMAN, BUSINESS CONSULTANT

You've poured enough milk on your cereal when the edge of your pile of Cheerios first starts to move.
MIKE RAMBO, PHOTOGRAPHER

About one fifth the cost of producing a book is the cost of the paper.
MARSHALL LEE, BOOKMAKER

The distance between your fingertips, with your arms outstretched at shoulder height, is equal to your height.
C. Dees, Trivia Buff

One acre will park a hundred cars.
E. Mankin, Journalist

A stolen painting will sell for one tenth of what it would sell for on the open market.
Ken Dalton, Artist

It takes three tries to get a new idea right, especially if a physical prototype is involved. The first try reveals any obvious shortcomings, and the second try cleans these up so you can see what you really need to do.
J. Baldwin, Designer and Writer

Optical paradoxes

Visual contradictions stimulate the mind. Here is one of my favorites, the wheel which doesn't know which way it's turning.

Haiku

The traditional Japanese form of poetry — Haiku — consists of three lines adding up to 17 syllables. Although the verses can seem terse, their purpose is to paint simple portraits of life, of the change in seasons, of the moments of silence in life. Haiku gives us a moment to look at some thing, or some event, and see it more clearly than we have seen it before. Perhaps we can see and feel what these Japanese poets saw and felt.

Old pond ...

a frog leaps in

water's sound.

Basho

the voice of the pheasant;

how I longed

for my dead parents!

Basho

autumn clear

the smoke of something

goes into the sky.

Shiki

The book of questions

In *The Book of Questions*, author Gregory Stock presents a series of questions to challenge the soul. Consider some of these:

- Your house, containing everything you own, catches fire; after saving your loved ones and pets, you have time to safely make a dash and save one thing. What would it be?

- Relative to the population at large, how would you rate your physical attractiveness? Your intelligence? Your personality?

- Does the fact that you have not done something before increase or decrease its appeal to you?

- What is the worst psychological torture you can imagine? Anything causing even minor physical injury should not be considered.

- What things are too personal to discuss with others?

How big is a million?

- A million is about the number of words in three spy novels.

- A million seconds is about eleven and a half days. (A billion seconds is about thirty years.)

- A million inches is just under sixteen miles, about the diameter of a city with a million people.

- A million dollars earns $2,740 interest each day.

- A million gallons of water would flow across Niagara Falls in one and three quarter seconds. It is also enough water for a town of about 28,000 people to take a bath.

Eggification

How can you make an egg stand on its end?

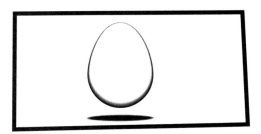

Napoleon's solution was to tap the egg slightly on one end, making a small depression. No one ever told Napoleon that he couldn't break the rules.

The three-dimensional dots

It's possible for some people to look at two pictures side by side, cross their eyes, and merge them into a single three dimensional image. Below is a collection of random dots. But if you merge them into a single picture, something remarkable happens.

Palindromes

These phrases read the same backward as forward.

Madam, I'm Adam.

A man, a plan, a canal, Panama!

Live not on evil.

Never odd or even

Step on no pets.

Pull up if I pull up.

Now sir, a war is won.

Was it a can or a cat I saw?

Niagara, O roar again!

Sex at noon taxes.

"Desserts!" I stressed.

The paradox

A paradox is a statement which incorporates the elements of self-reference, contradiction and a viscious circle. Like a snake biting its own tail, paradoxical ideas give us endless reflection.

- Please answer yes or no to the following question: "Will the next word you speak be no?"

- It is forbidden to forbid.

- This sentence is false.

- I imitate everyone except myself, Pablo Picasso

- In 1765, the government of Hapsburg Vienna published a catalogue of forbidden books. In 1777, the catalogue had to be included in its own contents because people were using it as a guidebook of interesting reading.

- The mystery of life is like a safe in which the combination is locked up in the safe.

SIDE ONE

The statement on the other side of this card is false.

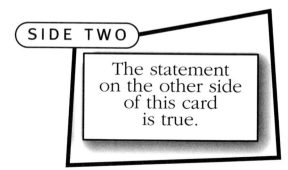

SIDE TWO

The statement on the other side of this card is true.

Bulls

Bulls are foolish wisdom — statements and stories which initially seem to make sense, then foolish, then meaningful in their nonsense.

- To a foot in a shoe, the whole world seems paved with leather.

- Set out from any point. They are all alike. They all lead to a point of departure.
  ANTONIO PORCHIA

- No snowflake ever falls in the wrong place.
  ZEN

- The future is but the obsolete in reverse.
  VLADIMIR NABOKOV

- A throw of the dice will never abolish chance.
  MARCEL DUCHAMP

- If you think you're free, there's no escape possible.
  RAM DASS

- Beware, as they say, of mistaking the finger for the moon when you're pointing at it.
  JOHN CAGE

- Each moment is a place you've never been in.
  MARK STRAND

- Between yea and nay, how much difference is there?
  LAO TZU

- There is no reason why a kaleidoscope should not have as much fun as a telescope.
  MARK TWAIN

- Nothing is more imprecise than precision.
  EUGENE IONESCO

- The greatest enemy of any one of our truths may be the rest of our truths.
  WILLIAM JAMES

- Be obscure clearly.
  E.B. WHITE

- In order to compose, all you need to do is to remember a tune that nobody else has thought of.
  ROBERT SCHUMANN

- Light is the shadow of God.
  RELIGIO MEDICI

- Two pyschologists meet. One says, "You're feeling fine, how am I?"

Step one

Lead your thinking in new directions by posing these questions:

- What are three "what if" questions you can ask?

- How can you involve other senses in developing your idea?

- Can you incorporate dreams into your thinking?

- What strange, bizarre and off-the-wall things can you do to develop your idea?

Step two

Look at your idea from brand new perspectives:

- Are there any rules you can break?

- Are there any new rules you can make up?

- What other names can you give your idea?

seasoning

Keep your ideas alive by continuing to search, examine and probe. There's no better way of doing this than to have fun, fool around and look at the strange side of life. Creative thinking means never having to say it's too strange.

Tip one

Collect interesting ideas, quotes, pictures, games, stories, puzzles and paradoxes. These make life interesting and shift your focus toward the little ingenuities of life. Ask "what if?" questions to help you look beyond conventional boundaries.

Tip two

Change mental languages. Try to express your idea using words, images, music, equations and physical movements. Flip modes of thinking to understand your project better.

Tip three

Cultivate luck. Be on the look-out for things which you can incorporate into your project. When something bad happens, ask yourself, "what good can come of it?" Sometimes nothing will. But if you don't look deeper, you might miss a discovery that will change the world.

taste

evaluate ideas

the taste test

Here are three clock faces.
What do you think about them?

the refined palate

EVERYTHING OF IMPORTANCE HAS BEEN SEEN
BY SOMEONE WHO DID NOT DISCOVER IT.

Alfred North Whitehead, Essayist

Once you've gathered, chopped up, mixed, cooked and spiced ideas into a creative feast, what do you do next? In both cooking and creative work, you taste to evaluate your results. You determine those ideas which are great, those which need to simmer more, and those which should be dumped into the trash. Tasting means paying critical and close attention and deciding if the thing does what you want it to do.

Judgment is itself a creative activity, and it occurs throughout the creative process. During the course of his or her work the writer asks, "Is this the right word or phrase," the artist ponders, "What should go into the bottom left corner of the canvas," and the city planner wonders, "What are the consequences of this decision?" Looking closely, listening attentively and touching sensitively, the creative person continually weighs the value of ideas.

But because there are no clear, fixed rules of evaluation, people can be too critical or too accepting in their judgments, and both extremes yield unfortunate results. Too critical, and you can kill a good idea before it gets off the ground; too tolerant and you risk wasting time on impractical, pie-in-the-sky ideas.

Consider what might have been the consequences if these people had been the final arbiters over ideas:

"With regard to the electric light, much has been said for and against it, but I think I may say without contradiction that when the Paris Exhibition closes, electric light will close with it, and no more will be heard of it."
ERASMUS WILSON, OXFORD PROFESSOR, 1899

"Heavier than air flying machines are impossible."
LORD KELVIN, CHEMIST, 1885

"The horse is here to stay, but the automobile is only a novelty — a fad."
THE PRESIDENT OF THE MICHIGAN SAVINGS BANK ADVISING HENRY FORD'S LAWYER NOT TO INVEST IN THE FORD MOTOR COMPANY, 1893

"Who the hell wants to hear actors talk?"
HARRY M. WARNER,
PRESIDENT OF WARNER BROTHERS PICTURES, 1927

"Everything that has been invented has been invented."
CHARLES H. DUELL,
COMMISSIONER OF THE U.S. PATENT OFFICE, 1899

When are people not discerning enough? Sadly for us, many brilliant innovators also devoted considerable energy to unrewarding studies. The great German astronomer Johannes Kepler spent a great deal of his time writing about astrology. Alfred Russel Wallace, Darwin's rival who independently developed the theory of evolution through natural selection, spent his final years trying to communicate with the dead: he wanted to prove that the spirit world speeded up the evolution of humans from apes. The biologist Francis Joseph Gall, who first showed that different parts of the brain performed different functions, also developed phrenology, the theory that a person's mental capacity was reflected in the shape of his or her skull. Who can say what contributions these thinkers might have made had their thoughts not have taken such unfortunate detours?

We need to strike a balance when judging the fruits of creative labor so that we neither stifle imaginative thinking nor allow the flow of ideas to run out of control. To do so, we must first discover which way we lean in our own evaluations. Here's a test. Between 1962 and 1977, Mr. Arthur Paul Pedrick, of the *One-Man-Think-Tank Basic Physics Research Laboratories of 77 Hillfield Road, Selsey, Sussex*, patented 162 inventions. None of these patents was ever developed commercially. What do you think of them?

Underwater travel

This modified bicycle could be ridden on dry land, on wet land and underwater. It could be used in the monsoon season in southeast Asian countries, and to transport scuba divers. However most scuba divers can swim much faster than they can ride a bicycle underwater.

Slice and cut adjuster

A golf ball which could be steered in mid-flight. (This broke the rules of the game and never made it into the mainstream golf world.)

Backseat driver

This contraption allowed a driver to operate a car from a back seat. Handy if you wanted to play a joke on traffic police, but of little other practical use.

Relay irrigation

Perhaps Pedrick's most ambitious invention was a scheme to irrigate the deserts of the world by sending a constant supply of snowballs from the polar regions through a network of giant peashooters.

For most people, the knowledge that none of these
inventions ever went anywhere provides sufficient evidence to support tossing them all into the wastebasket. But wait. Perhaps we could use the underwater bicycle for gentle physiotherapy. Or find military applications for the steerable golf ball.

In fact, people are generally more inclined to dismiss ideas than to nurture them. This is a problem inherent in the very word "criticism," which implies finding fault. When asked to think critically about an idea, we tend to look for the negatives. Judgment becomes an act of concluding: we identify good and bad ideas and dismiss the bad ones. This, however, suppresses the creative mood. Rather than concluding, then, evaluation should be a redirection. If something is good, it makes it to the top of the active list of ideas. If it is not so good, it is assigned a lower priority. Whenever the idea sits, tasting should still allow for the discovery of new possibilities, for making adjustments and for borrowing, combining and recombining options.

There are two basic approaches to judging. There is the logical, left-brain approach in which we compare results with objectives. If an alternative fulfills our declared objective, we're on the right track. If it doesn't, we need to examine other possibilities. In this process, we invite criticism, make plans for future improvement and grade our work.

And there is the intuitive, right-brain approach in which we trust our gut feeling and listen to some invisible sixth sense. We'll choose to go with an idea (or not go with it) because it feels right (or doesn't feel right). We decide on something new because — well, just because.

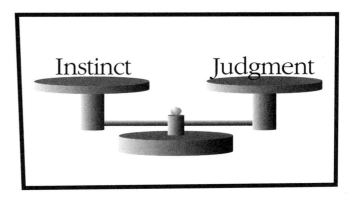

Should we follow the voice of reason or the voice of intuition? Are the best judges those who proceed logically or those who decree by insight? Of course, we need to use both. If we limit ourselves to only one of these approaches, we restrict the tools we have at our disposal. As Henri Jules Poincaré once asserted, "It is by intuition that we discover and by logic that we prove." By being aware of both, applying our analytical powers and exercising our intuition, we can arrive at clearer, more informed and more satisfying judgments.

logic

What might a critical judge who relies solely on logic say about the clockfaces in the opening exercise? He or she might raise the following objections:

The faces aren't circular.

It's hard to tell time at a glance.

The hands are hard to see.

They are really different from "real" clocks.

Why would anyone buy them?

Are these criticisms reasonable? Absolutely. Are they objective? Maybe. Do they inspire further creative thought? Not likely. The limitation of these judgments is that they evaluate in a single context — in this case, the conventional notion that clocks are circular with twelve divisions and two or three hands. But what if the clocks were designed to be tactile, read by sight-impaired people? Or what if the clocks were targeted to time-management consultants as conversation pieces? Or what if they were marketed simply to people with chaotic schedules?

Although these clocks don't fit our usual idea of "clockness," they are not necessarily failures. If we alter our definition of a clockface, our criteria for success change as well.

Using logic, we run into problems when we have unclear goals, ill-defined objectives or a lack of options. If we're just not sure about an idea, it may be time to return to our original vision, clarify our intentions and visualize the ideal outcome.

From the point of view of logical analysis, evaluating an idea means asking two key questions about it:

What's right with the idea?

What's wrong with the idea?

Teach yourself to focus on positive aspects first. Think of all the reasons the idea is a good one. There will be plenty of other people around to tell you why it won't work.

Consider using an idea checklist. Every product has its own kind of checklist. Here you ask questions which identify the idea's best features as well as those that will lead you to make improvements. The questions you apply to a love letter will be different from the ones you will use to determine the marketability of a video training program. Nevertheless, the following *Recipe* provides some general questions to get you started.

Step one

Write your idea at the top of a page.

Step two

Ask questions to help you define how good your idea really is:

What are your objectives?

If you haven't already done so, identify the criteria for success now. The more clearly you specify your intentions, the easier it is to evaluate your results. If you don't establish a clear destination, how will you know when you get there?

Is your idea effective?

Does the idea do what you want it to do? Will it save money? Get you a promotion? Double your free time? Make you happy? What steps can you take to enhance its effectiveness?

Is the idea an improvement?

Does your idea represent a step forward, or are you changing just for the sake of change. If the latter is true, is that prudent?

Is it timely?

Does your idea feel like it would work now? What is your competition thinking about now? Should you wait a few minutes, a few weeks, a few months or years? Or should you rush to market as soon as possible to get the first impact?

Is it practical?

Look at the idea from the perspective of the person responsible for the bottom line. It's all very well to come up with a plan for digging up minerals on the moon, but if the costs are prohibitive and likely to remain so, you may be better off setting the idea aside.

Is it simple?

In the fourteenth century, William of Ockham wrote a treatise called "Non Multiplica" which roughly translates into the phrase, "Don't make things unnecessarily complex." His principle of keeping explanations simple — now known as Ockham's razor — is as useful today as it was in the Middle Ages. Ask yourself: is the idea as simple as it can be? Is it direct? Can you write a two- or-three-sentence description which makes sense to everyone? What can you eliminate and still be successful? Use the KISS (Keep It Simple, Stupid) rule whenever possible.

Is it human?

Is your idea compatible with human nature? Could your mother use it? *Would* she? Remember that even though people may be capable of doing something, they may resist — even when logically, they're better off doing it.

Is it elegant?

How does your idea fare when measured against such aesthetic principles such as harmony, contrast, balance and unity?

Step three

Devise several other questions which relate specifically to your idea.

1. _____ ?

2. _____ ?

3. _____ ?

4. _____ ?

5. _____ ?

more analytical techniques

Checklists are not the only analytical techniques at your disposal. You can also evaluate an idea or situation using a numerical measuring scheme. Draw a line and mark off numbers from zero to ten. Then consider your subject: Where is it now? Perhaps your relationship with your boss is two or five. Ask yourself what will need to happen in order for the relationship to become a six? Or an eight? Or a perfect ten? The analytical line can be applied to any product or experience. Imagine how you might use it to develop your product, manage stress or add zest to your life.

Instead of a number line, you may prefer to use other ranking systems such as stars, grades or percentages. The principle is the same for all of them. Locate your current position and determine what you need to do to make it to the top.

If your work needs an objective evaluation, try bringing in a group of nonpartisan advisers. Look for people with different backgrounds and areas of expertise. Get suggestions, not approvals. People know when you are being sincere and are really looking for solutions. Here are some of the questions you might want them to answer:

- What decisions do you need to make about your project?

- Are you solving the real problem?

- When you confront new ideas, initially focus on the positive aspects. What's right about the idea?

- Is your timing right?

- In what ways could the project fail? Where are the weaknesses?

Checklists, ranking schemes and outside observers help us measure and compare ideas — when all the facts are in place. But what happens when we don't have all the information?

trust in your intuition

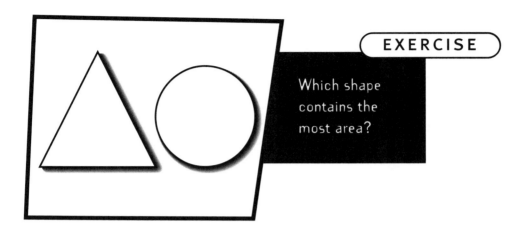

Which shape contains the most area?

What happens when you need to make a decision but don't have enough information? What do you do when you need to plot a course of action but circumstances are changing quickly and dramatically? During these times you need to trust your gut instinct.

Most schools teach us not to trust our intuition. The educational system focuses on right and wrong, on solitary correct answers and on proper responses to multiple choices. But after we leave the textbooks behind, we need to call on our thoughts, feelings and sensations to solve problems. Often, we're unprepared. Here are a few exercises to get you into the habit of calling on your instincts to help with decision making.

Get in touch with your gut

The first step is to learn to recognize your instincts. Take two sheets of paper. On one, write down the word YES. Think about how you feel when "yes" is the answer. Recall a few times when you have felt clearly and definitely positive about an idea. Note them down.

Identify three basic features of your gut feeling of "yes." On the second sheet of paper, do the same thing for NO. What are the signs when your instincts are telling you to stop, to avoid or to change direction on a project?

Ask, "How do I feel about the idea?"

Give yourself room to have many feelings about the idea. Set a quote if you have to. Be open to your feelings. Accept that they have as much legitimacy as logical reasoning.

Is there a metaphor for your gut reaction

If your idea was an article of clothing, how would it feel? Well worn and comfortable, or scratchy and stiff? Would it fit you well? Choose any metaphor from page 137 and apply it to your idea.

Coin a term

Video-game developers use an expression to describe a great game. It's got to be "simple, hot and deep."

Simple, so that anyone can learn quickly. Hot, so that it's exciting. Deep, so that it's constantly interesting and challenging. Come up with a term or expression which sums up your idea.

trust your gut

If the information is still incomplete, and despite calling on your instincts, a decision continues to elude you, try the technique of calling in an imaginary expert consultant.

Choose a problem that you are currently facing. Select a panel of expert consultants. What would these people have to say to you?

You can even engage the services of an expert through visualization. In your mind, invite one or two people in, who you imagine could help you solve your problem. If yours is a religious issue, invite Jesus, Buddha, Mohammed or Moses. If yours is a problem of creativity, call Beethoven, Einstein, Leonardo da Vinci or Groucho Marx. If it's a political problem you face, call Machievelli or Winston Churchill. In the privacy of your own mind, share your dilemma with them and hear what they have to say. They're experts, they've been through similar situations in the past, and best of all, they're free of charge.

Often what you need to do to train yourself to be more sensitive to your intuition is to give it expression. One way is to visualize possibilities and then check your emotional response. Albert Einstein flipped a coin, and then immediately asked himself, "How do I feel?" Then he would go with the gut reaction.

A very good way to focus your intuitive imagination is to pose your question in the language of intuition — images and sensations. For example, if you need a yes/no answer, pose the question and visualize the word "yes" in regard to that particular question. Think of it as a tangible entity, with a definite size, material, temperature. I've seen many people use this scheme and seen a wide variety of answers. The most interesting images appear in people's imaginations. People see heavy metal blocks, or slippery, almost ethereal letters. The way each image appears is a clue to the way your intuition conceives of the significance of each answer.

redo, rewrite, revise

Criticism alone is not enough. The person who evaluates but who doesn't fix will never progress. Once you've critiqued the idea, the next step is to improve it.

Making changes is as much a part of creative labor as is gathering ideas and working from inspiration. The point is easily missed, though, because we rarely see what artists have discarded or what form their ideas first took. By the time the product gets to us, long hours have been spent revising, polishing and getting it just right. As you spend these seemingly thankless hours honing your idea, take comfort in the knowing that Beethoven composed countless musical passages which never went beyond his notebooks. Hemingway rewrote passages four or five times — sometimes more — before he was satisfied with them. Many television commercial are shot 20 times or more before they make it to the screen.

One of William Strunk Jr.'s strongest pieces of advice to writers — and most forcefully delivered — was, "Omit needless words! Omit needless words! Omit needless words!" Strunk stressed that sentences should be simple, direct and to the point. In *The Elements of Style* he wrote, "Vigorous writing is concise. A sentence should contain no unnecessary words, a paragraph no unnecessary sentences, for the same reason that a drawing should have no unnecessary lines and a machine no unnecessary parts. This requires not that the writer make all his sentences short, or that he avoid all detail and treat his subjects only in outline, but that every word tell." The Swiss designer Arni Raia recast this rule for writers in a universal form, saying:

"Less is more."

Often we become so attached to our work that we resist letting anything go. We've worked so hard and been so closely involved that we cling to the results and become blind to the possibility of doing things any other way.

But for the sake of the work, we must be able to stand back, take an objective look, and ruthlessly discard anything that interferes with our progress toward the ideal. Just like freeing a caged bird, we must remove the bars and wires so that our idea can take flight.

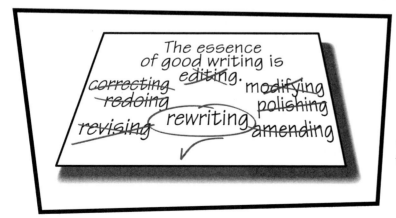

The essence of good writing is editing. ~~correcting~~ ~~redoing~~ ~~revising~~ rewriting modifying polishing amending

what can you simplify?

According to a famous anecdote, Albert Einstein was once asked why he always used hand soap for shaving, rather than shaving cream. The brilliant physicist replied, "Two soaps? That is too complicated!"

Although we might dismiss this story as a reflection of eccentricity, it illustrates a value central to Einstein's creative genius. He had a powerful inclination to simplify. In the introduction to his famous 1905 paper which introduced his theory of relativity, he wrote that he was inspired to develop his ideas not because of some new experimental evidence, but because of an asymmetry — an inelegance — in the equations relating electricity and magnetism. For Einstein, the fact that two different sets of equations were needed to describe a single principle was clumsy. In his search to simplify, he developed a new theory of electrodynamics.

Ellen Nearing, an American pioneering homesteader, expressed this idea another way:

If a recipe cannot be written on the face of a 3 x 5 card, off with its head!

The best solutions are simple ones. If your work is taking on Rube Goldberg-esque proportions, you can be reasonably certain that you've taken a wrong turn somewhere along the line.

what is blinding you?

Sometimes our worst enemy is the idea which we know all too well. It stops the deeper stages of developing original thinking. If we enter into a problem situation carrying the solution, no matter how much we say we are going to analyze and "be objective" about this thing, we still know that we don't have to work too hard at it because there's always one way out of the dilemma, and we have it in hand.

How can I capitalize on limitations

The food engineers at your corporation have developed a very tasty and nutritious breakfast cereal which is deep purple. Devise a marketing plan for this product.

Gut response

Which of these three designs do you like better? Why? How would you change them?

And & and & and

You and a partner open a consulting firm. Which ampersand do you choose for your logo?

After two years you decide (together) to open a cheese shop instead. Now which ampersand is best.

More time passes, fortune smiles upon you and your shop grows into a mighty food conglomerate. Which ampersand do you go with this time?

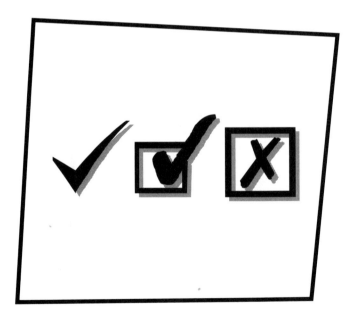

the joy of failure

"THE MOST IMPORTANT THING THAT THE NATIONAL COUNCIL ON THE ARTS CAN DO IS TO GIVE THE CREATIVE MIND THE RIGHT TO FAIL. IT IS ONLY THROUGH FAILURE AND THROUGH EXPERIMENT THAT WE LEARN AND GROW."

Isaac Stern, Violinist

Lucky for archaeologists, back in the third millennium B.C., the builders of the Saqqarra Step Pyramid realized that their pyramid design was too steep. If they continued to build at the same angle, the pyramid would collapse. The builders tapered the pyramid in mid-construction and it has stood the test of time. Two structures which weren't so fortunate were the Beauvais Cathedral and the Tocoma Narrows bridge. But though these structures were lost, they taught their builders valuable lessons about architectural design and the effects of wind, lessons which have been incorporated into building design ever since.

Failure is a natural part of the creative process. Even the greatest baseball player, with a batting average of 400, will fail at the plate six times out of ten.

Many people see failure as a sign of defeat, a penalty for wrong decisions, bad planning, sloppy execution. And though failure can be disheartening — and disastrous — it is a key part of the creative process, a necessary stepping stone to larger success.

Failure is just a basic fact of life for the creative individual. What really makes the difference is the person's response. Rodgers and Hammerstein's first musicals bombed and the two didn't work together for many years. Jonas Salk, who discovered the vaccine for polio believed, in retrospect, that he was on the wrong track over 98 percent of the time. Thomas Alva Edison discovered two thousand ways not to make a light bulb.

Yet, none of these people gave up. Determined, creative individuals can have their manuscripts rejected, see their plays flop and watch their computer programs crash without losing their tenacity. They accept failure as a necessary step toward refining their ideas. They keep track of their errors, learn from them and make adjustments until they get a product that works.

Many of us tolerate and even anticipate mishaps when we travel. Everyone has stories of disastrous holidays, of days when things just kept going wrong, where vacations turn into nightmares. The strange thing is many people delight in the misadventures. Long after we have forgotten the names of the hotels we stayed in or the directions to the museums, we remember the trials we endured.

But though we happily recount our misadventures during travel, we are less willing to accept failure in other aspects of our lives. I think one reason is that when we are traveling, we live a mind-set of adventure. We are eager for a challenge. Lost traveler's checks produce opportunities for us to live by our wits.

If you are always successful in everything you do, you are not getting the challenge necessary for real growth. Failure must not always be avoided. It is an important part of learning. Learning to fail — in definable, controllable ways — can deeply enhance the creative process.

quick failures

The goal is to increase quick failures. Paul MacCready, the inventor of the human-powered Gossamer Condor airplane says that his success is due to crude, fast and inexpensive experiments. By testing quickly, and on a small scale, he can minimize the damage and learn from his mistakes.

If the notion of embracing failure is bothersome to you, use different words which put a positive spin on the situation, such as challenge, insight or opportunity. Remember that success represents the one percent of your work that results only from the 99 percent which is called failure. There is an African proverb which says, "No one tests the depth of a river with both feet."

The American industrial designer Charles Kettering once said, "An inventor is simply a person who doesn't take his education too seriously. You see, from the time a person is six years old until he graduates from college he has to take three or four examinations a year. If he flunks once, he is out. But an inventor is almost always failing. He tries and fails maybe a thousand times. If he succeeds just once then he's in. These two things are diametrically opposite. We often say that the biggest job we have, is to teach a newly hired employee how to fail intelligently. We have to train him to experiment over and over and to keep on trying and failing until he learns what will work."

Failing intelligently means that you learn from what doesn't work. You think about the experience and change something. Foolish failure means you make the same mistakes over and over again, without learning anything new. The amateur approach is to hang onto your work and defend it. The professional knows better: if something doesn't work, you change it or you throw it out. Elbert Hubbard put it this way: "A failure is a man who has blundered, but is not able to cash in the experience."

Perhaps one of the most valuable contributions one can make to the creative culture of a company is to introduce the notion of failure — not large failures, but quick, relatively painless failures. Consider some of the following questions to encourage your thinking about the positive effects of failure:

What are the three biggest failures of your life? Why do you consider them failures? What could you have done differently to have prevented them?

What have you learned from your failures? Is there a message that you gave yourself as a result of these failures?

What failures are you moving toward now? Can you avoid them? What quick failures can you experiment with now to avoid potentially larger ones in the future?

Are there any kinds of failure that you can imagine enjoying?

What are the three biggest successes in your life? Why do you consider them successes? What did you do to make these experiences successes?

tasting

Tasting and judging help you sharpen and define your work. Making creative decisions about what to include and what to leave out, which direction to go and how to develop something, is a never-ending process. These decisions are reached through the dynamic pull and push of creative thinking: we need to be loose so that we don't stop good ideas prematurely, and we need to be critical so we don't serve a meal that's off.

Tip one

Reach a balanced judgment by involving both logic and instinct in your evaluation. Look for what's right about the idea before proceeding to what's wrong with it.

Tip two

Follow up on your evaluation by fixing the problems. Avoid becoming overly attached to an idea just because it's yours. Remember that revision is also a creative activity.

Tip three

Embrace failure and learn from it. If you are not willing to fail, even temporarily, you are probably not stretching your abilities as far as you might. The person who doesn't make mistakes usually doesn't make anything.

the loose ends

"PROJECTS ARE NEVER COMPLETED:
YOU ONLY FIND A TEMPORARILY INTERESTING PLACE TO PAUSE."

Wujec's maxim

Every project — every poem, painting, musical score, marketing plan — has good ideas which, for one reason or another, don't quite fit, which don't fall in line with the main theme of your work. In the development of any creative project, there are always loose ends. The question is, what should we do with them?

In researching this book, I came across many wonderful examples of creative works. The science of chaos, which studies order and disorder, has elements of creativity and spontaneity. And speaking of spontaneity, what about Chinese brush painting? Surely some discussion about the free-flowing painting is worthwhile in a book on creativity. What about juggling, performing in front of an audience or the mechanics of organizing one's material?

In writing this book, I explored several alternative paths. What happened to the chapter called SERVE? Isn't it important to talk about getting your ideas out the door, from the kitchen to the dining room? And where did that section on clichés go? Maybe I should have included excerpts of conversations with creative individuals? And shouldn't there be more about variations on a theme — which I've come to believe is the real crux of creativity. What about all those wonderful stories about innovators at work: Hermann Rorschach and his fascination with ink blots, for example; Srinivasa Ramanujan, the brilliant but impoverished Indian mathematician who was decades ahead of his time, formulating theories which are still being unraveled today.

And what about the other layouts I considered? No one will get to see them, or hear the other titles for the book. In the course of this project, I had to decide which loose ends should be picked up and tied to the main rope of ideas. There are always plenty of these types of decisions to be made, in every creative work, no matter which field.

Experienced creative individuals tell us that we shouldn't worry too much about the loose ends. There is a good chance that we can use them in the next project, or in the one after that. There will be time in the future to pick them up.

And if we don't get to them in the future, the threads bring us back to our starting point, a confrontation with disorder and the desire to make sense of it. We all have our own starting points of basic issues, of questions of meaning, sense of beauty and purpose. We can rest in the knowledge that we will return to these themes again and again, exploring them and reexpressing them, getting close to the ideal and then trying again. That's what catching the loose ends is all about.

digest

9

assimilate ideas

visualizing your creativity

SPEND A FEW MOMENTS RELAXING.

COLLECT YOUR ATTENTION,
AND ALLOW YOUR BODY, MIND AND BREATH
TO BECOME CALM AND RELAXED.

AS YOU FEEL YOURSELF BECOMING MORE TRANQUIL,
VISUALIZE YOUR CREATIVE SPIRIT.

WHAT DOES IT LOOK LIKE?
IS IT CONCRETE OR ABSTRACT?
DOES IT POSSESS COLOR, SHAPE OR SIZE?
IS IT MOVING OR STILL?
IS IT DIFFUSED OR SHARP AND WELL DEFINED?

HOW DO YOU FEEL AS YOU EXAMINE IT?

IS THERE ANYTHING "BEHIND" YOUR CREATIVE SPIRIT
WHICH SUSTAINS OR SUPPORTS IT?

WHAT DO THE ANSWERS TELL YOU ABOUT
THE SOURCE OF YOUR CREATIVITY AND INSPIRATION?

inner digestion

After all is said and done, after the long hours of preparation — gathering, cutting, mixing, cooking, spicing and taste testing — there finally comes a time to sit down at the table, clink glasses with your companions and enjoy the fruits of your labor. Taking time — however momentary or prolonged — to appreciate and to reflect completes the creative process. Reflective time extends the opportunity to take in, assimilate and digest the results of creative work, providing the room to further explore implications of new ideas, new feelings and to place new discoveries into perspective. Reflection generates the feeling of deep satisfaction.

Why is creative work satisfying? At one level, this question is easy to answer. Most often, creative successes come in the form of worldly accomplishments and met goals. Reaching a sales objective, completing a house addition, contributing to a family in need and perfecting an artistic rendition are all creative successes. They help to fulfill basic human drives — obtaining food, shelter, companionship, sex, among others. Yet at another level, the results of creative effort are more subtle.

Creative successes nourish the creative spirit. Each accomplishment encourages the mind and emotions, infusing them with excitement, confidence, vitality, depth and understanding. As we have seen throughout the *Five Star Mind*, there is room for creative expression in almost every domain of life, and this creative expression is as personal as we want it to be. Providing the room to assimilate allows us to reflect where our next personal creative challenge and opportunities may lie.

We can think of the creative spirit as a kind of energy which circulates through our mind, emotions and body. This energy continually flows and changes, expands and shrinks.

We can also think of the creative spirit as having two faces: the faces of invention and discovery. When the spirit of invention is strong, we become problem solvers, innovators and fabricators. Creativity becomes a tool for other purposes. Our orientation is to fulfill needs, to reach expectations and to reach goals. On this path, finding the solution takes priority.

When the spirit of discovery becomes most active, we become explorers, pioneers and revolutionaries. Creativity becomes an end in itself. Our orientation is not to reach goals, but to explore unknown territories, connect with the mysterious and find foreign lands. The spirit of discovery will delve into art form as deeply as possible, shaking things up and questioning the fundamental laws governing the art.

The spirits of discovery and invention live in all people. Although their orientations are quite different, they are nourished by similar properties. The creative spirit is nourished by novelty; each fresh experience provides wider outlooks and more breadth. The creative spirit is strengthened by well-honed skills; the more a person learns to command every aspect of his or her art and to understand his or her relationship to it, the more facility the creative spirit can flow. And finally, the creative spirit is nourished by passion; in fact, passion is the emotion which most characterizes the creative spirit.

mental indigestion

Look at any group of young children playing together and it is plain to see that their lives are filled with invention and discovery. Look at the same group 30 years later and these grown-up children have changed profoundly. Why have these children changed their focus from invention to rules? One reason is that when creative spirits are fed certain kinds of experiences, they gain a powerful case of mental indigestion.

The right way

According to creativity consultant Roger von Oech, the average person takes over 2,600 tests, quizzes and exams through the formal years of education. These tests package ideas in terms of right or wrong, correct and incorrect, and in neat multiple-choice boxes. But life is rarely so neatly arranged. While schooling helps us to take in new data, it does little to encourage us to explore, discover and create new ideas for ourselves. How often were you rewarded in school for challenging and doing something different?

Fear of failure

The risk of starting a new business venture, of leaving a familiar job, of submitting an unpolished manuscript, of exposing what you really think and feel is a gamble. Since there is always a chance of failure, courage has to play a role in putting new ideas into action. Risks makes people nervous. The person who is never willing to fail will never produce anything new. Being willing to be wrong gives you the freedom to embark into unexplored territory.

Fear of change

Many people associate creative minds with untrustworthy, unreliable, out-to-lunch, off-the-wall, weird wackos who can't fit in with society and do nothing more than rock the boat. This notion may stem from the fact that true innovators have to break down walls all the time. Since creative thinking involves change, and everyone resists change, innovation will often step on somebody's toes.

Intolerance of uncertainty

Creative minds embrace the feeling of uncertainty. To think creatively is to invite doubt, indecision and uncertainty. Although this sense of irresolution can produce anxiety and bring the flow of ideas to a dead halt, it can also produce a sense of excitement and progression. Time spent wavering, questioning and doubting should never be seen as wasted, but as part of a larger process.

Familiarity

The sidewalk in front of your home may not seem remarkable in any great way, but to a child, it is a landscape of possibility. The cracks are river valleys, the pebbles are boulders and the sidewalk extends into impossible distances. Similarly, a job, a house situation, a business endeavor can also become so familiar that you can't see the possibility of other ways.

The rules

Learning to follow the rules begins when we learn to color inside the lines. We work within the rules of society, of organizations, of proper ways of thinking and doing. The most difficult rules to break are those imposed by our own imagination.

Habits

A habit is simply the tendency to think, feel and do the same thing we have done before. From our life patterns to how we take off our shoes, habits direct all our actions. But doing something only because that's the way we've done it before does little to enhance creative potential. In fact, it only deepens the habit. Creative thinking — doing something new for yourself — involves a break with habit and the patterns of the past.

How do creative individuals change their diet from too many mental carbohydrates and sweets to one that is balanced and satisfying? First, by becoming aware of what they actually do consume; second, by reflecting on what they could consume, which would lead to satisfaction; and third, by ingesting what they know will nourish.

nourishing the creative spirit

"OUR PALATE WILL BE SHARPER, MORE ATTENTIVE TO NUANCE
IF IT IS ENTERTAINED, KEPT OFF GUARD,
GIVEN SOMETHING NEW EVERY FEW BITES.
CONTRAST AND VARIETY ARE BIOLOGICALLY CERTIFIABLE
CULINARY PRINCIPLES."

Harold Mcgee, Author

Through the course of this book we have examined many kinds of techniques to understand, explore and challenge our creativity. We have seen that our creativity is not a single feature of our minds. It is a rich resource which lives in our bodies, emotions and thoughts, and is expressed in endless ways. Creativity is a state of being, a muscle, a kind of energy, a disposition, an attitude, a collection of abilities. Because of this, the expression and growth of creativity becomes as unique as the individual.

Although we have seen many recipes for great ideas, we have also seen that there is no single recipe or plan for creative expression, other than perhaps doing what you love. The spirit of invention is nourished with challenges, needs to be filled, questions to be answered, solutions to be found, stories to be told and images to be painted. And there is no shortage of these kinds of challenges. The spirit of discovery is nurtured by becoming aware of the unknown. It responds to the realization that there may be new territory to be explored, just beyond the horizon. In any subject we explore, we will always find the mysterious: there are always horizons.

All people have something valuable to say. There is an inherent worth of all inner truths and the creative spirit is the power which can formulate and express these truths, connecting one person to the other. Each time a person completes a creative quest — a big "C" or little "c" creative — that person fulfills a little dream. All aspects of life have the potential of self-expression, even within tight deadlines. There is always room for experimentation, innovation and fun.

Knowing this, creativity becomes our ever-present companion and the creative spirit shines more and more brightly. Nourishing the creative spirit in others becomes the natural expression of our own spirit.

If ideas rule the world and determine its shape, creativity plants new ideas. And once planted, ideas grow, germinate and produce new ideas. And the cycle begins again.

"SINCE WE ARE DESTINED TO LIVE OUT OUR LIVES
IN THE PRISON OF OUR MINDS,
OUR ONE DUTY IS TO FURNISH IT WELL."

Peter Ustinov, Actor and Author

228

digesting

A creative moment is part of a longer creative process which, in turn, is part of a creative life.

Tip one

Stay loose, draw on the walls, read every day, imagine yourself as fire, laugh with kids, listen for the meaning behind the words, make dreams real, cultivate moods, play with anything you stumble across.

Tip two

Watch clouds, make friends with uncertainty, pay attention to spaces, unleash your imagination, put yourself on the line, get your hands dirty, refuse to compromise, do it for love and passion, trust in magic, practice concentration.

Tip three

Be kind, learn to juggle, look for heroes, feed whimsy, be solid as a rock, find openings, look elsewhere, notice the mysterious, zag when they zig, go with the flow, wait for something to happen, and when all else fails — make it up.

kayla's creative kitchen revisited

Before long, Tom had worked his way through the book and its recipes. He found the experience invigorating: it reminded him of the way he had once played as a child. But later, when he tried to apply the exercises to his daily life, he began to feel a sense of dissatisfaction. More often than not, one creative question led to another. Instead of generating tidy solutions to problems, creative thinking seemed to throw everything into doubt. Where life had once seemed clear and straightforward, there now seemed to be endless uncertainty.

For the first time in many years Tom felt unsure of himself, and he found this condition distressing. He confronted the problem one evening while he was taking the dog for its walk. Lost in thought, he wandered aimlessly, letting the dog decide where to go. After a while he looked up, and there, to his surprise, was the same sign he first saw from the end of the highway off-ramp. Tom was even more delighted to discover that the Kitchen was open, and that Kayla was sitting on her stool inside.

"Hello again," she called out cheerfully when she saw Tom. "What's cooking?"

"Not a lot," Tom answered. "But I'm in a stew."

Kayla laughed. "I see an improvement already. So what's the problem?"

Tom explained. "How do I stop myself from feeling this way?" he concluded.

"You don't. That is exactly the way you're supposed to feel."

"Well, I'm not sure that I like it."

"You won't — at first," Kayla explained. "What you're experiencing is creative tension. You're discovering what it's like not to know where you are going. People who are new to creative thinking don't like this feeling. They're used to quick solutions, and they're uncomfortable mucking around in the dark."

"Will this change, if I give it time?" Tom asked.

"In some ways, yes. You won't ever get over the feeling of risk. Any time you start a creative project — even a relatively simple one — you're putting yourself on the line. So there's always going to be a certain amount of anxiety and dread.

"But remember: great creative people don't have any less fear than you do. Some may even have more. The celebrated artist staring at a blank canvas and the famous actor peeking out at the audience before a performance feel the burden of their reputations weighing heavily on their shoulders.

"The difference is that with time and dedication, creative people learn to tolerate, appreciate and even love creative tension. They may not know where their work will lead them, but they are certain that the destination will be interesting. Some people even become addicted to creative anxiety: they live in a state of perpetual turmoil, feeling continually restless, empty and frustrated until they express their inner life in some creative way. Although, somehow, I sense that's not the life for you."

Tom grinned. "You've got that one right. But aren't you contradicting yourself? How can you know that you're going to be able to get things done and have doubts at the same time?"

"That's not necessarily a contradiction," Kayla answered. "Tell me, do you have any children?"

"Two. They're both in school now."

"All right. Think back to when the first was a baby. Didn't you have a lot of doubts back then?"

"You bet." Tom laughed. "We never knew if we were doing anything right. We must have bought a dozen books on feeding alone."

"But you never thought you wouldn't be able to raise a child. You always knew that somehow or other you'd muddle through. That's creativity for you. You work through the uncertainties, and your confidence builds with each success. The more you solve problems, find ways out of dead ends and discover inspiration when you thought you had exhausted all possibilities, the more you encourage creative anxiety to stir up new ideas.

"Now you're still new to creative thinking, so I'd recommend that you use moderation. Learn to manage your creative flame. If you start feeling overwhelmed, limit the number of creative projects you're working on. And here, take this card. When you need inspiration, pull it out and think about what it says."

Tom was relieved. He knew he would not be paralyzed by creative tension again. He thanked Kayla and said good night. His step was lighter as he made his way home, and instead of staring blankly at the cracks in the sidewalk, he looked with new interest at the buildings he passed.

And the card? What was Kayla's parting message?

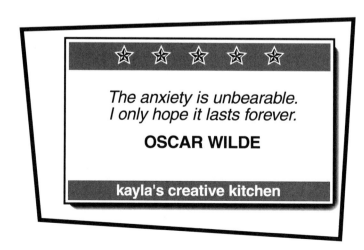

The anxiety is unbearable.
I only hope it lasts forever.
OSCAR WILDE

kayla's creative kitchen

solutions

answers to puzzles, quizzes and exercises

Word Puzzles

1 Just under the wire

2 Balanced budget

3 Standing ovation

4 Shot in the dark

5 Space in vaders

6 Bottom of the ninth

7 Sitting on top of the world

8 All hands on deck

9 Skinny dipping

10 Love at first sight

11 Canceled check

12 Dashed hopes

13 Splitting headache

14 Three square meals a day

15 Open sesame

16 Crossroads

17 Man overboard

18 Teenybopper

19 Seven seas

20 One in a million

21 Unfinished symphony

22 Once upon a time

23 An eye over the others

24 Two p's in a pod

25 Shape up or ship out

Cube

Hold the cube in such a way that one corner points toward you and the opposite points away from you; the cube's edges will form the outline of a hexagon. In this orientation, you will see there is plenty of room to pass through a cube face first.

Balancing Act

The answer can be obtained through a process of substitution. Work through the puzzle by substituting the weight of the shapes. A circle plus a square weigh the same as a triangle. One square weighs as much as a circle and a star. Two triangles weigh as much as three stars. Since a triangle equals a circle and square, then two circles and two squares equal six stars. By substituting a circle and star for each square, it turns out that six stars equal two stars and four circles. Therefore, a star equals one circle. Therefore, one square balances the weight of two circles.

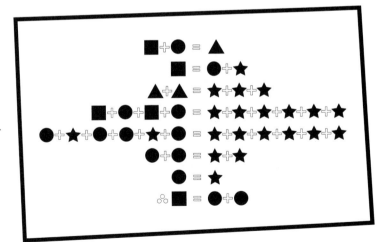

Tricky Cross

With diligence, you should be able to find a total of 21 squares.

Sixteen Dots

You can connect the dots with six strokes in the following way:

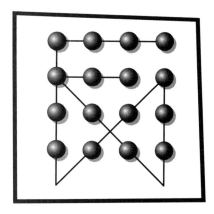

Tree Division

The plots of land can be equally divided in the following way:

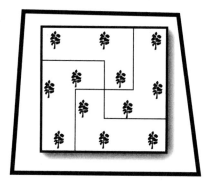

Shortest Route

The shortest route is to connect the houses in a snake-like pattern, as follows:

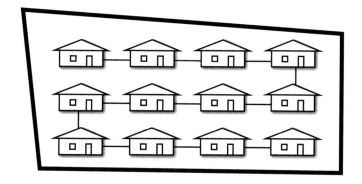

Unique Cube

There are 11 unique ways. If you unfolded the cube into six flat faces, here are the ways in which you could color them uniquely:

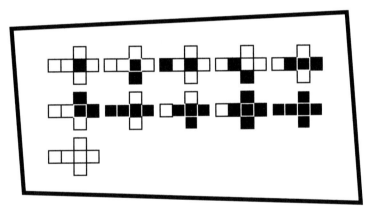

Simply Amazing

At every junction make a left-hand turn. This simple strategy will eventually bring you to the destination.

Tighter or Looser

The hole increases in size. Just think of what happens to a metal lid on a pickle jar when you run it under hot water.

Connecting

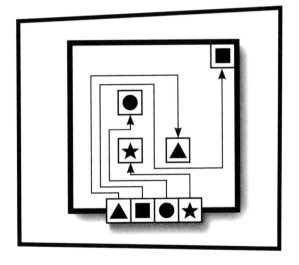

Close Call

The three mistakes are:
- The word "thre" is mispelled.
- The word "mistake" should be pluralized.
- The sentence has only two mistakes, which is the third mistake.

Visual Logic

The pattern is that each shape adds an additional right angle.

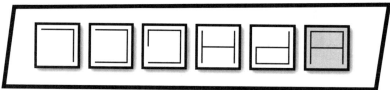

Single Strokes

The third shape cannot be drawn with a single stroke.

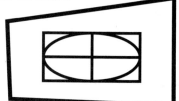

Mental Analysis

There are a total of 56 paths. Start at room A which as a starting point has one possible point of entry. For every other room, determine the number of paths into that room by adding the number of paths in the room above and the room to the left. Enter this sum into the room in question and continue to the next room until you have completed all the rooms. The sum in the lower right corner is the number of possible paths through the chambers.

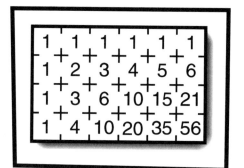

238

Behind the Scenes

There are 15 blocks in this figure.

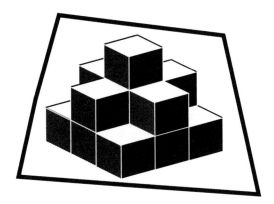

Squaring the Circle

First, cut the shape in the following way and rearrange the pieces into a square:

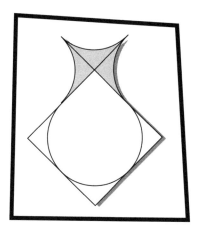

Exercise

You can arrange five coins so that each touches the other in this manner:

Mental Combination 1

This object is a disk with a slice out from one side.

Mental Combination 2

This object is a wedge with a smaller cube embedded inside. The trick is to orient the front and side views so they appear the same.

Mental Gymnastics

Seven twenty-fourths of the mixture is wine.

Clinking

You would hear 45 clinks. The general rule is to subtract one from the total number of glasses, then find the sum of all these numbers.

Rubber Squares

The following figure can be stretched into the first. This shape contains the same number of line connections as the circle figure

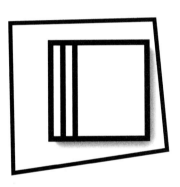

Connections

It is indeed possible to rearrange the nine dots into nine rows of three dots.

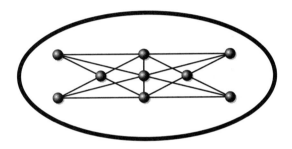

Connections

The "trick" is to pass one of the lines through one of the houses.

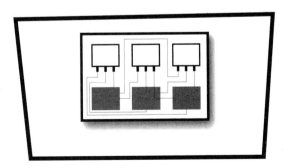

PAGE 126

Line Connections

Connect all twelve dots in five lines without taking your pen off the paper as follows:

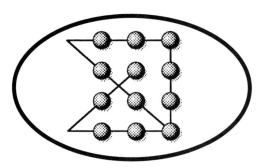

PAGE 127

Match Puzzles

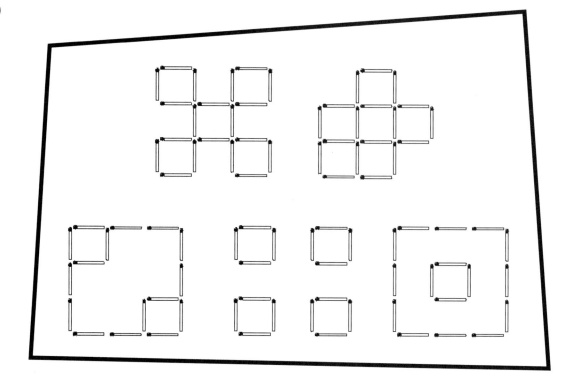

242

Four rows

You can rearrange two buttons in the illustration to create two rows with four buttons in each row as follows:

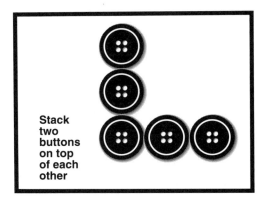

Stack
two
buttons
on top
of each
other

Intimate contact

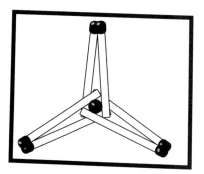

Lateral-Thinking Puzzles

The Amazing Shrinking Cup

Put your finger through the hole and push the cup.

Missing Bears

Each bear wore bandages and needed to stay in the hospital to get better.

New Word

The word is "Island."

PAGE 161

Trial and Error

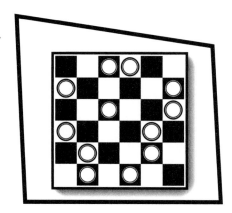

Mental Counting

There are 11 letters which contain curved lines, and 9 which are symmetrical. Curved letters: B, C, D, G, J, O, P, Q, R, S and U. Symmetrical letters: A, H, I, M, T, V, W, X and Y.

How Did They Do This

Begin with extra dominoes which support the bottom of the structure and remove them at the end.

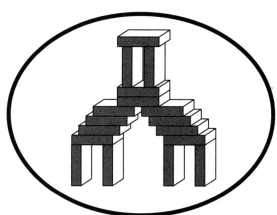

PAGE 186

Close Packing

It is possible to pack 12 balls three-dimensionally so that each touches the central ball.

about the author

Tom Wujec is Creative Director of the Royal Ontario Museum's Digital Media Services, where he develops interactive multimedia presentations, CD-ROM titles and new business ventures for the information highway. Tom has taught computer animation and brainstorming techniques and has produced a number of award-winning digital presentations. He also speaks internationally on the subjects of interface design and information design.

Tom is also author of *Pumping Ions: Games and Exercises to Flex Your Mind,* which has been translated into twelve languages.

We hope that you have enjoyed reading *Five Star Mind.* If you have any thoughts or experiences you'd like to share, please feel free to drop a line; we'd be delighted to hear from you.

If you would like more information about the CD-ROM version of *Five Star Mind*, which includes interviews from creative people — from brain surgeons to artists and from rock climbers to six-year-old girls who like to fingerpaint — as well as lots of interactive creative thinking activities to put on a Macintosh or Multimedia PC computer, we would also be pleased to hear from you.

You can address all correspondence to:

Tom Wujec

c/o Doubleday Canada Limited

105 Bond Street

Toronto, Ontario M5B 1Y3

Canada

or, if you prefer, you can reach Tom via the Internet at:
tomwujec@passport.ca

Photograph by Bently Quast